STUDENTS' MICROWAVE COOKBOOK

CAROLYN HUMPHRIES

foulsham
LONDON • NEW YORK • TORONTO • SYDNEY

foulsham

The Publishing House, Bennetts Close
Cippenham, Berkshire, SL1 5AP, England

Foulsham books can be found in all good bookshops or direct from
www.foulsham.com

ISBN 0-572-03137-8

Copyright © 2005 W. Foulsham & Co. Ltd

A CIP record for this book is available from the British Library

Printed in Great Britain by Cox & Wyman, Reading

CONTENTS

FEED ME

INTRODUCTION

FEED ME

Most of you will have used a microwave oven at home to reheat a meal when you've come in late at night, but you may not have realised it is the ideal machine to give you quick, tasty, nutritious and inexpensive meals now you're fending for yourself. It's small and fast, so uses the minimum of electricity, and if you are cooking for one, the less food you put in it, the quicker it cooks – unlike an ordinary oven where if you're bothering to heat it up you may as well cook a lot of food, otherwise you are wasting loads of fuel (for which, read 'money'!).

Most student accommodation has a microwave and, even if it isn't a brand spanking new, ultra-fast model, it will cook your food in record time. Here I give you some terrific meals for morning, noon and night – all great tasting, all so easy you could make them even if you've never cooked a meal before and, probably most important of all, they don't cost much!

HOW MICROWAVES WORK

I know this isn't a technical manual but, if you are going to get the best out of your microwave oven, it's a good idea to know how it works as it is very different from a conventional oven.

In an ordinary oven, heat is radiated around the food, cooking it from the outside inwards. This gives it the traditional brown, cooked appearance on the surface. In a microwave oven, the food is cooked by microwaves, which are similar to radio waves. These are converted from ordinary electricity using a magnetron, situated in the top of the microwave oven. The microwaves penetrate the food to a depth of about 5 cm/2 in. The waves cause the water molecules in the food to vibrate, producing friction, which creates the heat that cooks the food. However, because there is no external heat source, the food does not brown or crisp on the surface (you can remedy this by 'cheating', see pages 13–15).

Food reacts to microwaves instantly, so it cooks very quickly. Also, because the vibrating molecules cook the food, they don't immediately stop when you turn off the cooker; they continue to vibrate, gradually slowing down until they stop altogether. Therefore, food goes on cooking when the power stops or the food is taken out of the oven. This is why standing time is important as the food will complete its cooking during that time. You should never overcook food when microwaving; it should be slightly underdone when you take it out, then it will be cooked to perfection after the designated standing time. If you have miscalculated and it is still slightly undercooked, you can always pop it back in and give it a few more seconds. What you can't do is rectify a shrivelled, rubbery lump!

CONTAINERS AND EQUIPMENT

FEED ME

Another good thing about microwave cooking is that many of the dishes and bowls you would normally use just for serving food can also be used to cook food in.

You can use:
- ovenproof glass dishes
- specially made microwave ware
- glazed earthenware
- dishwasher-safe porcelain
- pottery and boilable plastic
- basketware and wood containers, but only for very short cooking such as warming bread rolls

Metal utensils, such as spoons or whisks, can be used to stir food – but never leave them in the microwave during cooking; leave a small plate by the cooker to rest any stirring spoons on. A wooden or plastic spoon, however, can be left in a bowl of food that needs repeated stirring during microwaving, but only for a short period of time. Also, make sure the spoon does not touch the top or sides of the oven during cooking.

You can't use:
- metal bakeware
- ironstone pottery
- thin plastics
- any crockery with a metal trim

The Dish Test

To test if a container is suitable for microwave cooking, stand a mug half filled with water in the dish to be tested. Microwave on High (100 per cent power) for 1 minute. If the dish feels cool but the water is hot, it is fine to use. If the dish feels hot and the water is cool, the dish has absorbed the microwaves and shouldn't be used. Don't even try to test a a metal dish – or even a china one with a gold or silver painted rim – it will cause arcing (the microwaves bounce off the metal, causing sparks to fly) and it could damage the magnetron.

The Right Size and Shape

The size and shape of a container is also important:
- Round, oval or rectangular dishes with rounded corners give the best results, because the microwaves are distributed more evenly.
- Using too small a dish could cause the food to bubble over, and it may also take longer to cook as it is so dense.
- Using too big a dish may overcook the food and make it dry.
- A shallow dish of food will cook quicker than a deep one.
- Choose straight-sided containers and, if a lid is going to be needed, a casserole dish (Dutch oven) is ideal (but you can cover with an ordinary plate instead).
- For vegetables choose a dish large enough to hold them in a single layer.
- For a recipe cooked in liquid, such as a casserole, leave about 5cm/2 in above the ingredients to allow enough room for it to boil.
- For cakes and other foods that rise, make sure the container is deep enough to allow for the extra height.

As I've just explained, microwaves only penetrate food to a depth of about 5 cm/2 in and the residual heat created cooks the food. But there are several other important principles to take into account when microwave cooking:

- Microwaving is not an exact science. The quality, thickness, size and shape of the foods all make a difference to how long they will take to cook. In this book you will be given approximate cooking times. Always undercook rather than overcook because you can always test and then cook a little longer if necessary. As you become more familiar with the microwave you use, you will quickly learn to tell how long foods will take and when they are cooked to perfection.
- The size and shape of the dish is also important (see Containers and Equipment, pages 7–8). Round or rounded-corner dishes allow foods to cook more evenly. Shallow dishes of food cook more quickly than deep ones.

- Dense foods take longer to cook. For instance, a jacket potato will take around 4 minutes, but a baked apple will take less than half that time. Also, a prepared dish that cannot be stirred will take longer to cook right through, as the heat cannot be redistributed during the cooking process.

- If cooking more than one item, the same amount of microwave energy has to be distributed through more food. There is less energy per item so the cooking time must be increased. For instance, although one jacket potato will take about 4 minutes, two will take 7–8 minutes, depending on the output of your cooker.

- Thicker parts of foods should be placed towards the outside of the dish. For example, arrange chicken drumsticks in a starburst pattern with the bones pointing towards the centre of the dish. Likewise with vegetables like broccoli, the stems take longer to cook than the flowery heads, so the florets should be arranged with the stalks outwards.

- Foods at room temperature will cook more quickly than those straight from the fridge or freezer.

- Foods with a high fat or sugar content will get very hot very quickly. They can burn, so cook carefully and avoid using plastic containers that could melt. Always handle with oven gloves or you could burn your hands.

- It is not usually necessary to grease dishes when cooking in the microwave except some puddings. If greasing is recommended, smear very sparingly with oil or butter or margarine. Too much fat would impair the finished dish.

- Most foods will not crisp and brown as they would in conventional cooking, but meat or poultry with a high fat content will naturally colour after about 10 minutes. Well-cooked bacon rashers and pork crackling will crisp on standing. Pastry will burn if overcooked and so will foods with a high sugar content, such as chocolate. Bread, on the other hand, softens when reheated but will go completely rubbery or hard if overheated. Seconds can be crucial.

- Add salt after cooking as it tends to toughen the fibres of meat and vegetables.

• Clean up a spillages or splutters in the oven immediately after use – not only because it will be easier to clean but also because it could extend the cooking time of the next foods you put in there. Your microwave oven won't differentiate between a chicken portion and a dollop of old curry sauce, so fewer microwaves will be directed at the chicken!

Stirring and Turning

Microwaves usually have a built-in turntable to turn the food while cooking to help distribute the microwaves more evenly. Alternatively, your oven may have paddles or stirrers hidden in the base or top of the oven to do a similar job.

It is vital that food is piping hot and cooked throughout before serving, so it is also important to stir and/or turn food manually during cooking to distribute the microwaves evenly. If you don't, you will have hot spots in your food where the microwaves have been concentrated or cold spots where they have not reached. All the recipes in this book tell you when to do this. Remember, too, always stir reheated drinks before sipping because the surface will always be scalding, even if the liquid is cooler underneath. Once stirred your drink will be evenly hot.

Timing

I stress that microwaving is not an exact science. The length of time a food will take to cook will depend on its size, shape, density, amount of fat and sugar, and even the size and shape of the dish it is cooked in.

Cooking times also vary from microwave to microwave as well as depending on the output of the oven. All the recipes in this book were tested in an 850 watt oven. If yours has a lower output, the cooking time will be slightly longer. Always cook for the shortest time given, then check and cook a little longer if necessary. The more you use your microwave, the more you will get used to how long specific tasks take in your model and can then cook more confidently for specific times. Make a note on the recipes in the book of how long it took in your oven.

Most foods can be cooked on High (100 per cent power). Occasionally a recipe will call for Medium-high (70 per cent power) or Medium (50 per cent power) because a gentler cooking is required. You may also find you get better results on Medium for reheating made-up dishes and for quickly warming bread, croissants etc. You'll use Medium-low (30 per cent power) for defrosting.

Quantities

In this book, most recipes are for one or two portions. (If you are cooking just for you and the recipe serves two, you can always reheat the second portion the next day – see Reheating, pages 24–7). If you want to cook a larger quantity, the cooking time will be different. Here are some general guidelines:

- Use a larger dish.
- If doubling the quantity increase the cooking time by a half, for example, if the recipe for two people took 6 minutes, allow 9 minutes for a quantity for four people.
- Always cook for less time than expected, then check and add on extra time in short bursts, testing as you go.
- Microwave ovens don't like cooking huge quantities. The microwaves need to penetrate as much of the food as possible, so there must be room to stir food or rearrange it. Cooking a large quantity of rice, for example, will mean it is likely to boil all over the oven because the bowl won't be big enough to contain it and it will clump together, even if you attempt to stir it.

Covering Foods

As a guide, foods that are covered when cooking conventionally also need to be covered when microwaving. General rules:

- A piece of greaseproof (waxed) paper or kitchen paper (paper towel) is ideal to prevent foods spluttering.
- Microwave-safe clingfilm (plastic wrap) helps keep moisture in. It is not recommended that you use ordinary clingfilm in the microwave any more. It has been found that the diezethyl-

hexedipate (DEHA) used in the manufacture to make it stretchy can pass into food during cooking, though it is not known to what degree this may be harmful. You must make sure that the clingfilm you use is suitable for use in the microwave. It will be stated clearly on the packaging. If there are no instructions for use in the microwave, do not use it. When using clingfilm, pierce it in several places or roll back one corner to allow steam to escape, otherwise it will billow up during cooking. Also make sure it does not touch the food during cooking. A dish with a lid is a good alternative or you can rest a plate over the top of the dish (which is cheaper than using clingfilm all the time too!).

- When cooking dishes containing liquids, a plate that fits over the bowl or container, or a casserole dish (Dutch oven) with a lid are ideal.

- For reheating plated meals, put the food on an ordinary dinner plate and cover with an inverted second plate or a casserole dish (Dutch oven) lid to prevent drying around the edges during heating. You can buy proper microwave plates with lids or microwave domes for this, but they are not essential.

- Don't cover cakes or breads when cooking.

- Don't use foil for covering as it is metallic. But because microwaves can't penetrate foil, you can use small smooth strips to shield wing tips, bone ends or thin parts of food that would otherwise overcook or dry out. This is called shielding. If you use too much or it is too crumpled, arcing will occur, which can damage the oven (see Maintaining Your Oven, pages 28–30). You can use foil to cover food, shiny-side in, when taken out of the cooker for its standing time before serving. It is ideal, for instance, for wrapping individual, cooked jacket-baked potatoes. They will then finish cooking and keep hot for up to an hour. But a top tip, if you like the skin of your jacket potato crisper, is to wrap it in kitchen paper (paper towel) instead.

Browning Foods

We are all 'programmed' to like the brown look of cooked foods. As this does not happen naturally in the microwave, there are various ways to cheat.

Use a browning agent to colour the food before, during or after cooking or a brown coating to give added texture as well as colour.

Meat and poultry

Before cooking, either:

- Brush or smear with melted butter or margarine or oil and dust with paprika. However, if you are cooking something with fatty skin, like chicken, there is no need to add the fat; just sprinkle with paprika.
- Brush or smear with equal quantities of water and tomato ketchup (catsup) or brown or barbecue table sauce. Or just smear with a little soy or Worcestershire sauce.
- Brush with warm honey, mixed with a good dash of soy sauce and a dash of bottled or fresh lemon juice.
- Quickly brown the surfaces of meat or poultry in a frying pan before transferring to the microwave to complete cooking (but I don't bother with that in this book because it takes extra time and makes dirty pans!).
- Dip in beaten egg, then dried or toasted breadcrumbs, toasted nuts or sesame seeds, crushed crisps (potato chips), cornflakes or branflakes or stuffing mix.
- Marinate in your favourite marinade before microwaving. Those that impart a rich colour (like ones containing soy sauce, tomato, brown beer or red wine) are particularly good.

Half-way through cooking:

- Brush with a sticky glaze: redcurrant jelly (clear conserve), shredless marmalade or a mixture of clear honey and wholegrain or Dijon mustard.

After cooking:
- Place under a preheated grill (broiler) for a few minutes to brown any toppings and crisp any skin. (This is also good to make a golden crust on any other savoury dish.)

Cakes and breads, etc.

Chocolate and coffee cakes will look fine anyway, but there are several options if you want to improve the final colour and appearance of your other bakes.

Before cooking, either:
- Use wholemeal flour rather than white (you may need a little extra liquid).
- Use brown sugar instead of white.
- Substitute 2 tbsp of custard powder for the same amount of white flour.
- Sprinkle the surface with ground cinnamon, chopped toasted nuts, toasted desiccated (shredded) coconut, toasted sesame, poppy or caraway seeds or chopped glacé (candied) fruits.

Half-way through cooking:
- Sprinkle with a mixture of demerara or light or dark brown sugar and chopped toasted nuts.

After cooking:
- Dust cakes or biscuits (cookies) with sifted icing (confectioners') sugar or coat in butter cream, icing (frosting) or melted chocolate.

Thawing food in a microwave is quick, economical and hygienic. Many microwaves now have automatic defrost. You select the item and the weight and it will pulse energy on and off, so that standing time is built in. Simply follow the manufacturer's instructions. Here are the general principles:

- Thawing is usually carried out at Medium-low (30 per cent power). Unlike when cooking on High, the timing varies very little whatever the output of your model.
- If thawing meat or other foods where you don't want to use the liquid that drips out, place on a microwave rack or an upturned plate with a container underneath so the liquid will drip or run away from the food.
- Thaw in short bursts only, with standing time in between, because, if you microwave for too long, the outside of the food will start to cook.
- Check food before the end of the thawing time and remember that it will continue to defrost during standing.

- When thawing a block of minced (ground) meat, scrape off the meat as it thaws on the outside and transfer it to a plate while the rest is being microwaved. Free-flow mince can be cooked from frozen.

- Break up casseroles, soups or other foods frozen in a block as soon as possible during thawing and move the still-frozen pieces to the edge.

- Ease pieces of food apart as they thaw to allow more even distribution of the microwaves. You will need to do this for chops, diced meat, sliced bread, bacon rashers (slices) etc.

- Don't try to defrost whole joints or poultry completely. Start the process, then leave at room temperature, wrapped in foil, shiny-side in, to finish thawing. Salmonella, a nasty form of food poisoning, can occur if the flesh starts to cook before it is completely thawed. Poultry portions, steaks and chops can be thawed completely.

- Protect bone ends and thin ends of meat, poultry or fish with tiny strips of smooth foil as they thaw, to protect them from beginning to cook while the rest of the food completes thawing. Don't use large pieces or arcing (sparks that could damage the magnetron) will occur.

- Put cakes, bread, pies and desserts on a piece of kitchen paper (paper towel) to absorb moisture as they thaw.

- Don't try to defrost cream desserts completely. Again, start the process with a very short blast at Medium-low (30 per cent power) (45 seconds for four frozen éclairs or 3 minutes for a whole frozen cream cake), then leave to stand at room temperature to finish thawing.

- Remove any metal twist ties or lids before thawing in the microwave.

- Vegetables can be cooked straight from frozen. Bags of frozen peas, for instance, can be cooked in their bag. Flex the bag occasionally to distribute the microwaves evenly. But for one, obviously, you just take out what you need (see page 22 for cooking instructions).

DEFROSTING AND COOKING TIMES

FEED ME

You may often have something in the freezer you want to cook and eat in a hurry. Here's a quick guide to defrosting and cooking individual portions. If you buy frozen ready-meals, specific instructions will be on the packet. If you have fresh stuff in the fridge, just refer to the last two columns for quick cooking. The exact cooking time will depend on the output of your machine.

* = Thawing time on Medium-low (30 per cent power).
** = Cooking time once thawed on High (100 per cent power).

Food	Quantity	Special instructions for thawing	Thawing time*	Cooking preparation	Cooking time**
Bacon rashers (slices)	6–8	If defrosting a pack of bacon, slit open the pack. Start to defrost. Peel off rashers as soon as possible before they start to cook. Turn the pack over frequently. Stop as soon as you can finish separating them.	2 mins	Lay chosen number side by side on a plate or microwave rack over a plate. Cover with a plate or greaseproof (waxed) paper.	45–60 seconds per rasher
Burgers (all types)	1 standard	Cook from frozen.		Place on a plate or microwave rack over a plate. Cover with a plate or greaseproof (waxed) paper. Brush quorn or veggie burgers with a little oil. Turn over once.	1–1½ mins
Casserole or stew	1 portion	Remove any foil packaging. Place in a microwave-safe dish. Break up as soon possible.	6–8 mins	Cover with a lid or plate. Stir once or twice during cooking, rearranging any large pieces of meat or chicken.	2½–5 mins

Food	Quantity	Special instructions for thawing	Thawing time*	Cooking preparation	Cooking time**
Chicken breast	1	Place on a plate. Unless individually wrapped, cover with another plate. Turn breast over half-way through defrosting.	2 mins	Dry with kitchen paper (paper towel). Brush with one of the suggested browning agents (see page 14) or wrap in 1 or 2 rashers (slices) of bacon. Cover with a plate or greaseproof (waxed) paper to prevent spluttering. Turn over half-way through cooking.	2–3½ mins (if wrapped in bacon add on an extra minute.)
Chicken portion	1	Place on a plate. Cover wing tip or leg bone end with a thin strip of foil. Turn portion over half-way through defrosting. Remove foil after thawing.	3 mins	Brush with one of the suggested browning agents (see page 14). Cover with a plate or greaseproof (waxed) paper to prevent spluttering. Turn over half-way through cooking.	2½–4 mins
Chilli con carne	1 portion	Remove any foil packaging. Place in a microwave-safe dish Break up as soon as possible.	6–8 mins	Stir once or twice during cooking	2½–5 mins

Food	Quantity	Special instructions for thawing	Thawing time*	Cooking preparation	Cooking time**
Chop	1	Place on a plate. Cover bone end with a thin strip of foil if protruding. Turn chop over half-way through defrosting. Remove foil after thawing.	3 mins	Brush with one of the suggested browning agents (see page 14). Cover with a plate or greaseproof (waxed) paper to prevent spluttering. Turn over half-way through cooking.	1½–5 mins
Lasagne	1 portion	Remove any foil packaging. Place in a microwave-safe dish or on a plate.	5–8 mins	Turn the plate once or twice during cooking.	2½–5 mins
Meat or chicken curry	1 portion	Remove any foil packaging. Place in a microwave-safe dish. Break up as soon as possible.	6–8 mins	Stir once or twice during cooking.	3–6 mins
Shep-herd's/ cottage pie	1 portion	Remove any foil packaging. Place in a microwave-safe dish or on a plate.	6–8 mins	Turn the plate once or twice during cooking.	3–6 mins
Vege-table curry	1 portion	Remove any foil packaging. Place in a microwave-safe dish. Break up as soon as possible.	6–8 mins	Stir once or twice during cooking.	2–4 mins

Quick Reference Cooking Guide for Basic Accompaniments for One

Food and quantity	Preparation	Cooking time on High (100 per cent power)
All-in-one vegetables (1 potato diced, 1 carrot peeled and sliced, a handful of frozen peas)	Mix together in a shallow dish and spread out. Add 3 tbsp water. Cover with a plate or clingfilm (plastic wrap) rolled back at one edge.	7–9 minutes, stirring twice until the potato and carrot are tender. Sprinkle with a pinch of salt, if liked. Leave to stand for 2–3 minutes. Drain.
Broccoli (6 florets)	Arrange with the stalks facing out in a shallow dish dish. Add 2 tbsp water. Cover with a plate or clingfilm (plastic wrap) rolled back at one edge.	3–4 minutes or until just tender. Sprinkle with a tiny pinch of salt, if liked. Leave to stand for 3 minutes. Drain.
Bulghar (cracked wheat) ($\frac{1}{2}$ mug)	Put in a bowl and add 2 mugs of water. Cover with a plate.	3–5 minutes until boiling. Leave to stand for 30 minutes.
Carrot (1 large)	Peel and thinly slice. Spread out in a shallow dish. Add 2 tbsp water. Cover with a plate or clingfilm (plastic wrap) rolled back at one edge.	3–5 minutes. Sprinkle with a pinch of salt, if liked. Leave to stand for 2–3 minutes. Drain.
Couscous ($\frac{1}{2}$ mug)	Put in a bowl and add 1 mug of boiling water or stock made with $\frac{1}{2}$ stock cube. Stir well. Cover with a plate.	4 minutes. Season with salt and pepper, if necessary. Stir well with a fork to fluff up. Can be left to stand if wished.
French (green) beans (a good handful)	Pull or cut off the tops and tails. Cut into short lengths or leave whole. Spread out in a shallow dish. Add 3 tbsp water. Cover with a plate or clingfilm (plastic wrap) rolled back at one edge. If frozen, cook straight from frozen.	3–4 minutes, stirring once. Sprinkle with a pinch of salt, if liked. Leave to stand for 2–3 minutes. Drain.

Food and quantity	Preparation	Cooking time on High (100 per cent power)
Jacket potato (1 large)	Scrub the skin and prick all over with a fork. Wrap in a piece of kitchen paper (paper towel).	4–5 minutes until soft when squeezed. Wrap in foil for a soft skin, leave in kitchen paper for a firmer one. Can be left to stand for up to an hour.
Pasta shapes (½ or 1 mug, depending on size of pasta)	Put in a large bowl with 2–3 mugs of water. Stir.	8–10 minutes, stirring twice, until just tender, but still with some 'bite'. Add a pinch of salt. Leave to stand for 2 minutes. Drain. **Note:** quick-cook varieties will take less time – the same as cooking conventionally, so check the packet.
Peas (frozen) (½ mug)	Place in a bowl. No water necessary.	2 minutes, stirring once.
Rice, long-grain (½ mug)	Put in a bowl. Add 1¼ mugs of boiling water. Stir well. OR Put in a bowl. Add 2–3 mugs of boiling water. Stir well.	8–10 minutes or until the grains are just tender. Add a pinch of salt. Leave to stand for 2–3 minutes until the liquid has been absorbed. OR As above, but drain well in a colander after standing and rinse with boiling water.
Spaghetti (a small handful)	Break the strands into 2 or 3 pieces so they will lie straight in the dish. Cover with plenty of boiling water. Stir.	About 8 minutes, stirring several times to loosen the strands, until just tender. Add a pinch of salt. Leave to stand for 3 minutes. Drain.

Many foods can be reheated successfully in the microwave. It is important to turn or stir food as appropriate to distribute the heat and to make sure that it is piping hot before serving, never just warm or even fairly hot.

Bought ready-meals nearly always have microwave instructions on them. Follow with care. Make sure you always remove any foil containers and empty canned foods into a microwave-safe bowl for heating.

General Instructions for Reheating Leftovers

- Put the food on a plate or in a bowl, if more suitable. Cover with a plate or a casserole (Dutch oven) lid.
- For foods that can be stirred (such as a casserole, chilli con carne, pasta or goulash), microwave on High (100 per cent power) for 3–5 minutes, stirring every minute, until piping hot. Leave to stand for 2 minutes before serving to distribute the heat evenly.

● For made-up dishes that can't be stirred (such as lasagne or cottage pie), microwave on High (100 per cent power) for 3–6 minutes until the base of the plate under the food feels piping hot. To test further, insert a knife down through the centre, wait 5 seconds, then remove. The blade should feel burning hot. If not, microwave a little longer. Leave to stand for 2–3 minutes before serving to allow the heat to distribute evenly.

Reheating Convenience Foods

Most of the following have microwave instructions on their packaging but here are some useful times and cooking tips.

Convenience food	Quantity	Special instructions	Cooking time (depending on power output)
Baked beans	1 × 225 g/8 oz/ small can	Empty into a bowl. Stir once or twice during heating.	1–2 mins
Baked beans	1 × 400 g/14 oz/ large can	Empty into a bowl. Stir once or twice during heating.	2–4 mins
Beans on toast	1 portion on 1 slice of toast	Make the toast in the usual way. Butter and place on a plate. Top with the beans.	1–2 mins
Hot dogs	2 cold hot dog sausages in 2 finger rolls	Wrap individually in kitchen paper (paper towel) and place well apart on a plate.	30–60 seconds
Leftover takeaway	1 portion 2 portions	Turn out of foil containers on to a plate. Cover with another plate or a lid. Stir gently twice during heating.	1½–3½ mins 3–6 mins
Meat or vegetable pie/pasty	1 individual	Remove from foil container, if necessary. Place on a piece of kitchen paper (paper towel) on a plate. The pastry will go soft; to crisp, after heating remove from the kitchen paper and put briefly under a preheated grill (broiler).	1–2 mins

Convenience food	Quantity	Special instructions	Cooking time (depending on power output)
Mince/fruit pie	1 individual	Remove from foil container, if necessary. Place on a piece of kitchen paper (paper towel). The filling will get very hot.	20–30 seconds
Pizza	1 × 20 cm/8 in	Place on a microwave rack to prevent the base getting too soggy or on a piece of kitchen paper (paper towel) on a plate.	2½–5 mins
Plated meal	Average plate of meat (or similar) and vegetables	Arrange the food with the densest pieces (such as potatoes) around the outside and the less dense ones (such as peas) in the centre. Make sure any meat is covered with gravy or a sauce or it will dry up. Cover with another plate or a casserole (Dutch oven) lid. Test that the food is hot through by feeling the centre of the base of the plate. If it is not very hot, microwave a little longer.	4–5 mins
Ravioli	1 × 400 g/14 oz/ large can	Empty into a bowl. Stir gently once or twice during heating.	2–4 mins
Sausage roll	1 medium	Place on a piece of kitchen paper (paper towel) on a plate. The pastry will go soft; to crisp, after heating remove from the kitchen paper and put briefly under a preheated grill (broiler).	15–20 seconds
Savoury mince	1 × 425 g/15 oz/ large can	Empty into a dish. Stir once or twice during heating.	3–5 mins
Soup	1 × 300 g/11 oz/ medium can	Tip into a large mug or bowl. Stir once during heating and once before serving.	1–3 mins

Convenience food	Quantity	Special instructions	Cooking time (depending on power output)
Spaghetti on toast	1 portion on 1 slice of toast	Make the toast in the usual way. Butter and place on a plate. Top with the spaghetti.	1–2 mins
Steak and kidney pudding	1 individual	Turn out of the can on to a plate. Cover with a large bowl.	1½–3 mins

Cleaning

- Always wipe up any spills straight after use or they will attract the microwaves next time you cook, which could affect the cooking time. Microwaves don't differentiate between food to be cooked and crumbs, messy dribbles or splutters.
- Wipe the inside with a dry cloth or kitchen paper (paper towels) to remove any condensation, which could cause rust in time. Make sure door seals are also kept clean or microwaves could escape.
- To freshen the interior (after cooking fish, for instance), put a bowl containing about a mugful of water, a few slices of lemon and a clean cloth in the oven. Cook on High (100 per cent power) for 3–5 minutes until boiling. Leave until lukewarm, then squeeze out the cloth and wipe all over the inside. Dry with a dry cloth or kitchen paper (paper towels).
- Never use scourers or oven cleaners in your machine.

Troubleshooting

If you think your oven is not working properly, there are several simple checks you can do before calling out an engineer.

1 Check the oven is properly plugged in.
2 Check the wires in the flex have not worked loose from the plug pins.
3 Check the fuse has not blown.
4 Check the oven door is shut properly.
5 Check the oven is not set to 'hold', 'timer' or 'auto'.
6 Make sure the air vent is clear and there is nothing heavy on top of the oven.

Safety

● Never switch on the microwave with nothing in it – it could damage it. To make sure this never happens, leave a mug of water inside the oven when not in use.

● Metallic utensils, large pieces of foil or crockery with gold or silver trims should not be used in the microwave oven as they reflect microwaves and will produce a blue spark called arcing. If arcing occurs, turn off the microwave immediately as it can cause serious damage to the cooker's magnetron. Arcing can also occur when very small amounts of food are being cooked. If this happens, place half a mugful of water in the cooker with the food. This will absorb some of the microwave energy and prevent it happening.

A Checklist of Dos and Don'ts for your Microwave

✓ Do read your manufacturer's instruction booklet properly (if you can find it!).
✓ Do make sure your oven is plugged in using a properly earthed, fused plug in a normal 13 amp socket.
✓ Do make sure the oven has an airspace behind it of at least 10 cm/4 in to allow air to circulate freely.
✓ Do use your normal household kitchenware for cooking and serving food. Make sure it is microwave-safe first (many dishes tell you this on their bases. If you are unsure, perform the dish test (see page 8).

✓ Do be careful about timing – every second counts. Cook for the shortest time given, then add on extra, a little at a time.

✓ Do remember that standing time for most foods is also important. It allows foods to complete cooking, so technically foods should be slightly underdone when removed from the cooker.

✓ Do use your microwave oven to its full potential to cook foods as well as thawing and reheating them and to warm drinks.

✓ Do cover foods when you are told to. This prevents drying out and spluttering in your oven.

✓ Do use thin strips of foil to protect thin ends of foods that could burn or dry out.

✓ Do keep your oven clean. Dirty surfaces will mean longer cooking times and dirty door seals could mean escaping microwaves, which could be potentially dangerous.

✗ Don't use metal containers or utensils in the microwave or large pieces of foil or metal ties.

✗ Don't use sealed containers as these could burst with the build up of steam.

✗ Don't cook eggs in their shells or re-heat hard-boiled (hard-cooked) ones: they will explode.

✗ Don't deep-fry foods in your oven: the oil temperature cannot be controlled.

✗ Don't turn on the oven when empty, it could damage it. Keep a mug of water in there when not in use to prevent this.

✗ Don't let thin strips of foil touch the interior of the oven.

✗ Don't try and dry wet clothes or papers in the oven. They might ignite!

✗ Don't put cans of food in the microwave.

✗ Don't attempt to dry fruit in the microwave: the high sugar content would make it burn before it is dried.

✗ Don't use the cooker if it is damaged in any way – especially if the door is loose or if the seals are faulty.

✗ Don't try and repair a microwave oven yourself. If the quick checks on page 29 don't work, call out an approved service engineer.

BASIC FOOD HYGIENE

FEED ME

A hygienic cook is a healthy cook – so please bear the following in mind when you're preparing food.

- Always wash your hands before preparing food.
- Always wash and dry fresh produce before use.
- Don't lick your fingers.
- Don't keep tasting and stirring with the same spoon. Use a clean spoon every time you taste the food.
- Don't put raw and cooked meat on the same shelf in the fridge. Store raw meat on the bottom shelf, so it can't drip over other foods. Keep all perishable foods wrapped separately. Don't overfill the fridge or it will run too warm.
- Never use a cloth to wipe down a chopping board you have been using for cutting up meat, for instance, then use the same one to wipe down your work surfaces – you will simply spread germs. Always wash your cloth well in hot, soapy water and, ideally, use an anti-bacterial kitchen cleaner on all surfaces too.

- Always transfer leftovers to a clean container and cover with a lid, clingfilm (plastic wrap) or foil. Leave until completely cold, then store in the fridge. Never put any warm food in the fridge. Don't store leftover canned food in the can – use a lidded plastic container.
- When reheating food, always make sure it is piping hot throughout, never just lukewarm (see Reheating, pages 24–7).
- Don't refreeze foods that have defrosted unless you cook them before returning them to the freezer.

STOCKING UP BEFORE YOU START

FEED ME

Many students persuade their parents or guardians to do a big shop for them before they start (or get them to take them out once they've unpacked and know what space is available for food). If you only have a tiny cupboard in a shared kitchen in halls, you'll have to make it pretty limited; but if you're sharing a house and intend to cook a lot, you can buy in plenty or pool resources with the other housemates.

All of the following are useful but, obviously, it's up to you and what you are likely to need. Use it as a guide only.

Ingredients to Keep in the Cupboard

- baking powder
- bottled lemon juice
- breakfast cereal
- bulghar (cracked wheat)
- cocoa (unsweetened chocolate) powder
- cornflour (cornstarch)
- couscous
- dried fruit – mixed, raisins, sultanas (golden raisins), apricots

- dried herbs – mixed, basil, bay leaves, oregano, parsley
- dried minced onion
- drinking (sweetened) chocolate powder
- flour – plain (all-purpose) and self-raising
- garlic purée (paste) – if you can't be bothered to crush fresh garlic cloves
- golden (light corn) syrup
- honey
- instant coffee
- jam (conserve)
- mayonnaise
- mustard – made English and Dijon
- nuts and seeds – peanuts, walnuts, caraway and sesame seeds
- oil – sunflower and olive
- pure orange and apple juice
- passata (sieved tomatoes) or tomato pasta sauce
- pasta – macaroni and/or other shapes, spaghetti, lasagne sheets, Chinese egg noodles
- pepper
- rice – long-grain, flavoured savoury
- salt
- sugar – caster (superfine) can be used for everything, but you could also buy granulated and light brown
- spices – chilli powder, cinnamon, ginger, cumin, coriander (cilantro), curry powder or paste, mixed (apple pie) spice, paprika
- stock cubes – beef, chicken, vegetable
- table sauces – brown, Tabasco or other chilli, tomato ketchup (catsup), soy, Worcestershire
- tea bags
- tomato purée (paste) (tubes keep best)
- vinegar – white wine or cider

Cans for Convenience

- baked beans (be wary of economy brands – too much juice and not many beans!)
- custard

- fish – salmon, sardines, tuna (check the label for 'dolphin friendly'; some brands are much cheaper than others and are still 'df')
- fruits – any are good, pineapple is very useful in cooking
- minced (ground) beef (great with pasta)
- pulses – red kidney beans (economy brands are good), cannellini beans etc.
- soup – condensed mushroom, celery, tomato (ideal for sauces)
- tomatoes (chopped are good for quickness in sauces but plum ones are cheaper – look out for economy brands)
- vegetables – sweetcorn, peas, carrots, green beans, mixed diced

Perishables

- bacon
- breads – rolls, pittas, tortilla wraps (store in the freezer if you have one, and take out when required; you can toast slices of bread from frozen)
- butter and/or margarine
- cheese – Cheddar and grated Parmesan, plus others as you need
- crème fraîche
- eggs, medium
- fresh fruit – apples, citrus, bananas
- frozen foods – peas, beans, spinach, fish and other seafood, minced (ground) beef or lamb (beware of economy mince, which may be very fatty)
- ham
- milk – keep a carton in the freezer so you won't run out; part-defrost in the microwave and shake well once defrosted
- vegetables, fresh – carrots, green vegetables, mushrooms, onions, (bell) peppers, potatoes, salad stuffs
- yoghurt – plain is good for sauces and dressings as well as for breakfast with cereal or with honey or fruit for dessert

NOTES ON THE RECIPES

FEED ME

- Measurements have been kept simple because I don't think many students want to be bothered with accurate weighing with measuring jugs, scales and so on. I've used an ordinary-sized coffee mug (not a giant one!) for wet and dry ingredients, ordinary spoons, not measuring ones, and handfuls of things like grated cheese.
- When measuring dry ingredients such as flour, it should be loosely packed, not pressed down firmly.
- American terms are given in brackets.
- The ingredients are listed in the order in which they are used in the recipe.
- Eggs are medium unless otherwise stated.
- Always wash, peel, core and seed, if necessary, fresh foods before use.
- Seasoning and the use of strongly flavoured ingredients, such as chilli and garlic, are very much a matter of personal taste. Taste the food as you cook and adjust seasoning to suit your own taste.

Should you, at a later date, want to use 'proper' measurements or if, for instance, you need to buy a block of speciality cheese for a recipe, these are the actual weights and measures I am talking about:

For liquid measures, 1 mug = 250 ml/8 fl oz

For large pasta shapes (e.g. shells or rigatoni), breakfast cereals (except muesli) and fresh breadcrumbs, 1 mug = 50 g/2 oz

For flour, bulghar (cracked wheat), small pasta shapes, diced fresh or frozen vegetables (e.g. peas), nuts and muesli, 1 mug = 100 g/4 oz

For couscous, lentils and dried fruit, 1 mug = 175 g/6 oz

For sugar, rice, butter and margarine, 1 mug = 225 g/8 oz

For grated cheese, dried fruit and nuts,
   1 small handful = 15 g/½ oz
   a handful = 25 g/1 oz
   a good handful = 50 g/2 oz

All spoon measurements are level unless otherwise stated: e.g. 1 tsp = approx 5 ml; 1 tbsp = approx 15 ml

- Fresh herbs – especially parsley, basil and coriander (cilantro) – really enhance lots of dishes. It's worth buying pots of growing herbs from the supermarket (they're not expensive) to keep on the windowsill – but don't forget to water them!
- Can and packet sizes are approximate and will depend on the particular brand.
- I tend to call for sunflower or olive oil in recipes but you can use any good-quality oil, like corn or groundnut (peanut), if you prefer. Avoid the really cheap unspecified vegetable oils as they don't taste that good, particularly for dressings.
- I call for butter or margarine in the recipes. If you use a spread such as sunflower, check on the tub that it is suitable for cooking as well as spreading.

- Use your own discretion in substituting ingredients and personalising the recipes. Make notes of particular successes as you go along.
- Remember, microwave cooking is very fast. Always cook for the shortest time given, then test and cook for a little longer if necessary.
- The clock symbol at the end of each recipe gives an estimate of how long it will take to make the dish from the start of preparation to the finish. Remember that the time needed will not only vary according to your microwave but also according to how long you take to prepare the ingredients – so it is only a rough guide!

BREAKFASTS

FEED ME

I've put these dishes together in the breakfast section because they are traditionally served at that time of day. However, every one of them makes great eating any time of the day or night when you fancy a light, easy snack meal.

MICRO BACON AND EGGS

I know traditionally students have fry-ups but this version is not only much better for you, it's also extremely quick.

Serves 1

2 rashers (slices) of streaky or back bacon, rinded
1 tomato, halved
A little oil for greasing
1 egg

1 Put the bacon rashers and tomato halves on a plate. Lay a sheet of kitchen paper (paper towel) loosely over the top. Lightly oil a saucer or small plate and break the egg on to it. Prick the yolk gently with the prongs of a fork.

2 Microwave the bacon and tomato on High (100 per cent power) for 1½–2½ minutes until cooked to your liking. Remove from the oven.

3 Cover the egg with another plate. Microwave on Medium–high (70 per cent power) for 30 seconds. Leave to stand for 1 minute. Remove the plate, then cook on Medium-high for a further 20–30 seconds until cooked to your liking.

4 Slide the egg on to the plate with the bacon and tomato and serve.

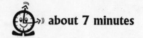 about 7 minutes

BAKED EGG WITH HAM

If cooking more eggs, use more individual containers rather
than cooking lots in one. Increase the cooking time per egg.

Serves 1

A small knob of butter or margarine
1 slice of ham, diced
1 egg
1 tbsp double (heavy) cream
Salt and pepper
To serve
Crusty bread

1 Grease a ramekin (custard cup), ordinary cup or very
small shallow dish with the butter or margarine. Add the
ham.

2 Break the egg into the dish and prick the yolk gently
with the prongs of a fork. Season with salt and pepper.

3 Spoon the cream over and season with a little salt and
pepper. Microwave on Medium–high (70 per cent
power) for 1–1 ½ minutes, then leave to stand for
2 minutes. If you like your egg hard, cook for a further
30 seconds.

4 Serve with crusty bread.

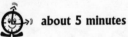 about 5 minutes

SCRAMBLED EGGS

Here's a recipe for plain scrambled eggs. Serve them on toast or try them with some of the variations given below.

Serves 1

2 eggs
2 tbsp milk
Salt and pepper
A small knob of butter or margarine

1 Break the eggs into a bowl. Add the milk. Beat with a fork or a wire whisk until thoroughly blended. Add a sprinkling of salt and pepper and the butter or margarine.

2 Microwave on High (100 per cent power) for 1½ minutes, stirring well once or twice, until scrambled but still slightly runny.

3 Leave to stand for 2 minutes to finish cooking. Stir again, then serve.

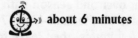 about 6 minutes

VARIATIONS:

Scrambled Eggs with Mushrooms

Slice two or three mushrooms and place in a bowl with the butter or margarine. Microwave on High (100 per cent power) for 1–2 minutes, stirring once, until cooked. Beat in the eggs, milk and some salt and pepper, then microwave as in the main recipe.

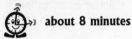 **about 8 minutes**

Scrambled Eggs with Kippers

Pierce the bag of a boil-in-the-bag kipper with butter. Microwave on High (100 per cent power) for about 3 minutes or according to the packet directions. Remove and leave to stand while you scramble the eggs as in the main recipe. Slide the kipper out of the bag on to a plate and serve with the eggs.

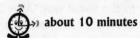 **about 10 minutes**

Scrambled Eggs with Bacon

Snip one or two rashers (slices) of bacon into dice with scissors. Place in a bowl and microwave on High (100 per cent power) for 1–2 minutes, stirring once or twice, until cooked through. Beat in the eggs and milk and a sprinkling of salt and pepper but omit the butter or margarine. Cook as in the main recipe and season to taste.

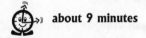 **about 9 minutes**

POACHED EGG FLORENTINE

This may sound a bit fiddly for brekkie but it doesn't take long. It is great brain food and will help fight fatigue too.

Serves 1

1 slice of bread
Butter or margarine
2 tbsp cheese spread
2 tbsp milk
1 mug frozen chopped spinach
2 tbsp water
½ tsp vinegar or lemon juice
1 egg

1 Toast the bread in the usual way. Alternatively, place it on a piece of kitchen paper (paper towel) and microwave on High (100 per cent power) for 2 minutes until crisp. Spread with a scraping of butter or margarine.

2 Mix the cheese spread with the milk in a small bowl. Cover with a plate and microwave on High for 2 minutes, stirring twice with a fork or a wire whisk, until hot and smooth. Remove from the oven and cover.

3 Put the spinach in a bowl and microwave on High for 2 minutes, stirring once.

4 Put the water and vinegar or lemon juice in a mug, cup, small bowl or ramekin (custard cup). Microwave briefly until boiling. Break in the egg and prick the yolk very gently with the prongs of a fork. Cover with clingfilm (plastic wrap), rolled back at one edge, or a plate. Microwave on Medium (50 per cent power) for 45–60 seconds until opaque. Leave to stand while you reheat the spinach and cheese sauce briefly in the microwave.

5 Press the spinach against the side of the bowl and drain off any liquid. Put the toast on a plate and top with the spinach. Using a slotted draining spoon, held over the sink, gently slide the egg out of its container into the spoon so the water drains away. Slide it on top of the spinach. Spoon the sauce over and serve.

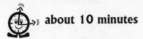 about 10 minutes

CHEESE AND MUSHROOM TOAST

If you want even more protein, microwave a couple of rashers of bacon (see page 19) before reheating at step 3.

Serves 1

1 slice of bread
1 tbsp soft cheese with chives
6–8 button mushrooms
A small knob of butter or margarine

1 Toast the bread in the usual way. Alternatively, place it on a piece of kitchen paper (paper towel) and microwave on High (100 per cent power) for 2 minutes until crisp. Spread with the soft cheese with chives. Put on a plate.

2 Wipe the mushrooms and place in a small bowl with the butter or margarine. Microwave on High for 2 minutes. Drain on kitchen paper.

3 Put the mushrooms on the toast and microwave for 30 seconds to reheat.

 about 6 minutes

TOMATOES ON HAMMY TOAST

This is quick to prepare and extremely delicious. Much more interesting than plain tomatoes on toast.

Serves 1

1 slice of bread
Butter or margarine
A little brown table sauce
1 slice of ham
1 large tomato, sliced
Pepper

1 Toast the bread in the usual way. Alternatively, place it on a piece of kitchen paper (paper towel) and microwave on High (100 per cent power) for 2 minutes until crisp.

2 Spread with a scraping of butter or margarine, then the brown sauce. Put on a plate.

3 Top with the slice of ham, then arrange the tomato slices over the surface. Sprinkle with pepper.

4 Microwave on High for 1–1½ minutes until the tomatoes are cooked.

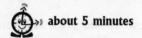 about 5 minutes

MICRO OMELETTE WITH HERBS

Go for variety by adding a small handful of grated cheese, diced ham, chopped tomato or sliced mushrooms.

Serves 1

A knob of butter or margarine
2 eggs
1 tbsp water
Salt and pepper
½ tsp dried mixed herbs
2 slices of bread and butter or margarine
Tomato ketchup (catsup) or brown table sauce (optional)

1 Put the butter or margarine on a dinner plate with a lip (not one that's completely flat) or a shallow dish. Smear it all over.

2 Beat the eggs with the water in a bowl with a fork or a wire whisk. Mix in a sprinkling of salt and pepper and the herbs. Pour on to the plate or into the dish.

3 Microwave on High for 1½–2 minutes, lifting and stirring the mixture twice during cooking, until the egg is set.

4 Sandwich between the slices of buttered bread, adding a dash of ketchup or brown sauce, if liked, and eat while still hot.

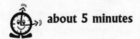 about 5 minutes

PORRIDGE

Ring the changes by adding a handful of dried fruit, a chopped apple or a mashed banana to the cooked porridge.

Serves 1

½ mug porridge oats
1 mug milk and water mixed (or all water)
A pinch of salt
To serve
Milk and honey

1 Mix the porridge oats with the liquid in a bowl large enough to allow for it to bubble up. Add the salt and stir well.

2 Microwave on High (100 per cent power) for 4–5 minutes, stirring twice, until thick and creamy. Serve with milk and honey.

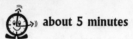 about 5 minutes

---

Re-crisp breakfast cereal

If you find half a packet of cereal that was left open at the back of the cupboard so the flakes are no longer really crisp, you can restore it!

1 Spread out the cereal in an even layer on kitchen paper (paper towel) on a plate.

2 One portion will take 30–45 seconds on High (100 per cent power). Stir half-way through heating. If necessary, heat a little longer until the cereal feels crisp. For larger quantities, microwave in 30 second bursts until crisp, stirring frequently. Leave to stand until cold, then store in an airtight container.

HOT MEGA MUESLI

Muesli makes an excellent breakfast but it can be like trying to chew through bird food. Cooking it is the perfect answer.

Serves 1

½ mug any bought muesli
¾ mug milk, plus extra for serving
1 eating (dessert) apple, chopped
A pinch of mixed (apple pie) spice (optional)

1 Mix the muesli and milk in a bowl, then stir in the apple and spice, if using.

2 Microwave on High (100 per cent power) for 4 minutes, stirring once or twice, until hot and thickened but still with some texture. Serve with extra milk poured over.

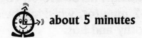 about 5 minutes

HONEY NUT CROISSANT WITH HOT CHOCOLATE DUNK

Sinful, decadent and delicious – the perfect comfort breakfast. Take care you don't overheat the croissant.

Serves 1

3 heaped tsp drinking (sweetened) chocolate powder
1 mug milk
1 croissant
1 tsp clear honey
1 tsp chopped mixed nuts

1 Whisk the drinking chocolate into the mug of milk with a fork or a wire whisk. Microwave on High (100 per cent power) for 1½–2 minutes, whisking twice during heating, until frothy and hot.

2 Put the croissant on a plate and trickle the honey over, then sprinkle the nuts on top. Microwave on High for 15–20 seconds. Serve hot with the hot chocolate, dunk and enjoy.

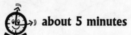 about 5 minutes

HOT FRUIT SALAD WITH YOGHURT

Dried fruit salad is fantastic brain food and will help you stay alert all morning. It's worth soaking it overnight.

Serves 1

½ × 250 g/9 oz packet dried fruit salad,
or a single dried fruit such as prunes or apricots

⅔ mug cold black tea or water

A good pinch of mixed (apple pie) spice or ground cinnamon

A large spoonful of plain yoghurt

---

1 Empty the fruit into a bowl and add the cold tea or water. Ideally, leave to soak for at least 15 minutes, preferably overnight.

2 Sprinkle the spice over the surface. Cover with a plate and microwave on High (100 per cent power) for 4–5 minutes, stirring once, until plump and juicy. Leave to cool for 5 minutes, then top with the yoghurt and serve.

 about 11 minutes, plus soaking time

SNACKS AND LIGHT LUNCHES

FEED ME

Microwave ovens are ideal for making almost instant snacks and quick meals. Here's a whole range of tasty ideas to choose from, whether you need fast food at lunchtime before a long afternoon lecture or want a quick snack late at night after the pubs shut. Whenever you need a light bite, you'll find something here to fit the bill.

NO-NONSENSE MINESTRONE

This is nutritious and filling. You can add other veggies, such as a bit of shredded cabbage.

Serves 2–3

1 onion, finely chopped
1 potato, finely chopped or coarsely grated
1 carrot, finely chopped or coarsely grated
A handful of frozen peas
A small handful of macaroni or spaghetti, broken into short pieces
1 × 400 g/14 oz/large can of chopped tomatoes
1 tbsp tomato purée (paste)
A pinch of dried oregano
A good pinch of sugar
1 vegetable stock cube, crumbled
Salt and pepper
To serve
Grated Parmesan or Cheddar cheese

1 Put everything except the salt and pepper in a large bowl. Fill the tomato can with water and add to the bowl. Add a second canful of water. Stir.

2 Cover with a lid or plate and Microwave on High (100 per cent power) for 15–25 minutes (depending on whether you've grated or chopped the veggies), stirring every few minutes, until everything is tender.

3 Season to taste. Leave to stand for 5 minutes, then serve in bowls sprinkled with grated cheese.

 » about 25–35 minutes

CHEESY-TOPPED FRENCH ONION SOUP

Traditionally this has slices of French bread coated in Gruyère cheese on top, but this is cheaper and easier!

Serves 1

1 largish onion, sliced or chopped
A good knob of butter or margarine
2 tsp sugar
½ beef or vegetable stock cube
1 mug boiling water
½ tsp soy sauce
Salt and pepper
1 slice of bread
A handful of grated Cheddar or Edam cheese

1 Put the onion in a fairly large bowl with the butter or margarine. Microwave on High (100 per cent power) for 4 minutes, stirring once or twice.

2 Stir in the sugar and microwave on High for 6 minutes, stirring once or twice, until soft and a pale golden colour.

3 Crumble the stock cube and stir it into the onions with the water and soy sauce. Microwave on High for 2 minutes. Season to taste.

4 Meanwhile, toast the bread and put on a plate. Alternatively, wait until the soup is cooked and place the bread on a sheet of kitchen paper (paper towel) on a plate and microwave on High for 2 minutes until crisp. Sprinkle the cheese on top.

5 Microwave on High for about 40 seconds until the cheese has melted. Cut into quarters.

6 Ladle the soup into a bowl and top with the quarters of cheesy toast.

about 15 minutes

CARROT AND ORANGE SOUP WITH CORIANDER

This fast and tasty soup will impress your friends as well as you. Keep a pot of fresh coriander on your windowsill.

Serves 2

1 × 300 g/11 oz/medium can of sliced carrots
1 mug pure orange juice
½ vegetable stock cube
2 tsp dried minced onion
½ tsp ground cumin
1 tbsp chopped fresh coriander (cilantro)
Salt and pepper
To serve
2 tbsp of crème fraîche (optional) and crusty bread

1 Empty the carrots including their liquid into a large bowl. Mash with a potato masher or fork. Add all the remaining ingredients except the salt and pepper.

2 Microwave on High (100 per cent power) for 4 minutes until boiling, stirring twice.

3 Season to taste. Serve topped with a spoonful of crème fraîche, if liked, and crusty bread.

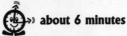 about 6 minutes

SWEETCORN AND POTATO CHOWDER

This is just too much for one person, so cool the remainder, store it in a container in the fridge and eat within 3 days.

Serves 2

1 potato, peeled and cut into small dice
1 small onion, chopped
A knob of butter or margarine
2 tbsp water
1 tbsp plain (all-purpose) flour
1½ mugs milk
1 chicken or vegetable stock cube
A good pinch of dried mixed herbs
1 × 200 g/7 oz/small can of sweetcorn
Salt and pepper
1 rasher (slice) of streaky bacon, rinded, (optional) or a small handful of grated Cheddar cheese

1 Put the potato and onion in a fairly large bowl with the butter or margarine and the water. Microwave on High (100 per cent power) for 5 minutes, stirring twice.

2 Stir in the flour, then the milk. Crumble in the stock cube and add the herbs.

3 Microwave on High for 5 minutes, stirring twice, until slightly thickened and the vegetables are tender.

4 Add the contents of the can of sweetcorn and season to taste. Microwave on High for 1 minute.

5 If using the bacon, remove the soup from the microwave. Cut the bacon into pieces and spread it out on a plate. Cover with a sheet of kitchen paper (paper towel). Microwave on High for 1 minute or until crisp.

6 Ladle half the soup into a bowl. Add the bacon or cheese and serve.

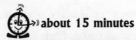 about 15 minutes

THAI NOODLE SOUP

You can use more noodles for a more filling meal. Or add a handful of chopped cooked ham for the last minute.

Serves 1–2

1 ½ mugs water
1 chicken stock cube
½ tsp minced lemon grass from a jar or grated lemon zest
A pinch of ground ginger
1 tsp soy sauce
¼ slab of fine Chinese egg noodles or 1 vermicelli nest
To serve
Thai rice crackers or bread

1 Put the water and stock cube in a bowl with the lemon grass or lemon zest, the ginger and soy sauce. Heat on High (100 per cent power) until the stock is boiling. Stir to dissolve the stock cube.

2 Break the noodles or vermicelli into small pieces and add to the stock. Continue to microwave for 5 minutes.

3 Taste and add a dash more soy sauce, if liked. Serve with Thai rice crackers or bread.

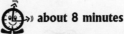 about 8 minutes

SPICED PEA DHAL WITH POPADOMS

This is so easy to make but makes an interesting dip with some fresh vegetables or a salad.

Serves 1

2–4 popadoms (or as many as you want to eat!)
1 small onion, finely chopped
A small knob of butter or margarine
2 tsp curry paste or powder
1 × 225 g/8 oz/small can of pease pudding
1 tsp tomato ketchup (catsup)
A small handful of raisins
A little bottled or fresh lemon juice
To serve
1 tomato, quartered, a few slices of cucumber and a wedge of lettuce

1 Microwave the popadoms, one at a time, on High (100 per cent power) for 45–60 seconds, turning once, until puffy all over. Repeat with as many popadoms as you want.

2 Put the onion and butter or margarine in a small bowl. Cover with a plate or a piece of kitchen paper (paper towel) and microwave on High for 2 minutes, stirring once or twice.

3 Stir in the curry paste or powder and microwave on High for 30 seconds.

4 Stir in the pease pudding, ketchup and raisins. Microwave on High for 2 minutes until piping hot, stirring once or twice.

5 Sprinkle with a dash of lemon juice and serve with the popadoms and a side salad of the tomato, cucumber and lettuce.

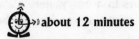 about 12 minutes

CHILLI DOGS

Store the rest of the hot dogs in their liquid in a covered container in the fridge for up to three days to eat cold.

Serves 1

2 canned hot dog sausages
2 finger rolls
2 heaped tsp chilli relish
2 tsp Dijon mustard

1 Drain the hot dogs on kitchen paper (paper towels). Prick with a fork.

2 Split the rolls but not right through. Spread inside with the relish and mustard. Put a hot dog in each.

3 Wrap each in a piece of greaseproof (waxed) paper or kitchen paper and place well apart on a plate.

4 Microwave on High (100 per cent power) for 30–60 seconds. Check that the dogs feel piping hot; if not, microwave in 10 second bursts. Don't overcook or the rolls with be tough and leathery! Unwrap and serve.

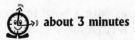 about 3 minutes

FAST BROWN BANGERS WITH ONIONS

If you fancy bangers in a hurry, here's a way to have them in just a few minutes – and nicely browned too!

Serves 1

1 onion, sliced
A small knob of butter or margarine
1 tsp sugar or clear honey
Salt and pepper
2 thick pork sausages
1 tsp soy sauce
¼ tsp paprika
To serve
Bread rolls or slices of bread, mustard and tomato ketchup (catsup)

1 Put the onion in a small bowl with the butter or margarine, sugar or honey and a sprinkling of salt and pepper. Microwave on High (100 per cent power) for 5 minutes, stirring twice, until soft.

2 Meanwhile, prick the sausages all over with a fork and place on an upturned small plate over a larger plate (to allow the fat to drip off). Mix the soy sauce with the paprika and spread all over the sausages.

3 At the end of cooking the onion mixture, cover it and leave to stand while you cook the sausages.

4 Cover the sausages with a bowl to prevent spluttering and microwave on High for 1 minute. Turn over, re-cover and cook for a further minute until cooked through and browned.

5 Place the sausages and onions in rolls, or split the sausages lengthways if you're using slices of bread, and serve with mustard and ketchup.

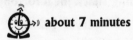 about 7 minutes

CIDER RAREBIT

If you have a dash of beer, lager or wine lurking, you can use it instead of cider. For non-boozers, use apple juice.

Serves 1

1 heaped tsp plain (all-purpose) flour
2 tbsp cider
3 tbsp milk
A knob of butter or margarine
A pinch of chilli powder
A good handful of grated Cheddar cheese
Salt and pepper
1 slice of bread

1 Mix the flour with the cider in a bowl until smooth, then blend in the milk. Add the butter or margarine, chilli powder and cheese. Microwave on High (100 per cent power) for 2–2½ minutes, stirring twice, until thick, smooth and bubbling. Add salt and pepper to taste.

2 Meanwhile, toast the bread. Put it on a plate.

3 Spoon the cheese mixture over the toast and serve.

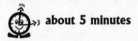 about 5 minutes

NACHOS

This makes a great nibble for a couple of friends or quite a filling snack meal for one.

Serves 1–2

1 × 225 g/8 oz/small can of red kidney beans
1 tsp dried minced onion
A good pinch of chilli powder (or to taste)
1 tsp tomato purée (paste)
A pinch of caster (superfine) sugar
Pepper
1 × 40 g/1½ oz/small packet of plain corn tortilla chips
A good handful of grated Cheddar cheese

1 Mash the kidney beans with a potato masher or fork in a bowl. Work in the onion, chilli powder, tomato purée and sugar. Season with pepper.

2 Spread a little of the bean mixture on each tortilla chip. Arrange them on a large shallow dish that will fit in the microwave, around the edges of the dish rather than in the centre.

3 Sprinkle liberally with the cheese and microwave on High (100 per cent power) for 2 minutes until the cheese has just melted. Serve straight away.

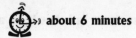 about 6 minutes

QUICHE IN A ROLL

You can leave one to get cold and have it for lunch the next day. Wrap it well and store it in the fridge once cold.

Serves 1–2

2 large crusty rolls
Softened butter or margarine
1 small tomato, chopped
1 slice of ham, chopped
2 good pinches of dried basil
2 small handfuls of grated Cheddar cheese
1 egg
4 tbsp milk
Salt and pepper

1 Cut the top off each bread roll. Pull out and discard most of the soft bread to leave a 5 mm/¼ in thick wall.

2 Spread the insides of the rolls with a little butter or margarine. Place well apart on a plate.

3 Divide the tomato and ham between the two rolls and add a sprinkling of dried basil, then the cheese. Don't pack it down hard, you want the egg mixture to be able to run through it.

4 Beat the egg with the milk and a little salt and pepper, using a fork or a wire whisk, until well blended. Carefully pour into the rolls, taking care it doesn't overflow.

5 Microwave on Medium-high (70 per cent power) for about 5 minutes or until almost set. Leave to stand for 3 minutes to complete cooking.

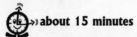 about 15 minutes

HOT PASTRAMI ON RYE

This is traditionally made on rye bread but this crunchy crispbread version is extremely tasty – and much cheaper.

Serves 1

A good knob of butter or margarine
2 gherkins (cornichons), chopped
2 rye crispbreads
2 slices of pastrami
A little Dijon or English mustard

1 Mash the butter or margarine with the gherkins and spread on the crispbreads. Top with the pastrami, then a scraping of mustard. Place on a plate.

2 Microwave on High for 40 seconds or until the pastrami is sizzling and the butter has just melted. Eat straight away while the crispbreads are still crisp.

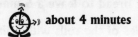 about 4 minutes

BARBECUED SAUSAGE BAGUETTE

You can cheat even more and use bottled barbecue sauce if you have some in the cupboard.

Serves 1

1 sandwich baguette
1 tbsp mayonnaise
2 thick pork sausages
1 tsp tomato ketchup (catsup)
¼ tsp clear honey
¼ tsp vinegar
½ tsp brown table sauce
A handful of shredded lettuce

1 **Split the baguette not quite right through and spread with the mayonnaise.**

2 **Split the sausages lengthways with a sharp knife and open out flat.**

3 **Mix the ketchup with the honey, vinegar and brown sauce. Spread all over the sausages on both sides.**

4 **Place the sausages rounded-sides up on an inverted small plate over a large plate, so that the fat runs down (unless using extra-lean sausages, in which case just put them on a plate). Cover the whole lot with an inverted bowl.**

5 **Microwave on High (100 per cent power) for 2 minutes. Place in the baguette and fill with lettuce.**

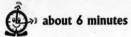 about 6 minutes

PIZZA BAGELS

Bagels are great vehicles for loads of toppings. They also keep quite well, so are worth having in the breadbin.

Serves 1

1 bagel, split in half
1 tbsp tomato purée (paste)
A good pinch of dried oregano
A good handful of grated Cheddar or Mozzarella cheese
1 tomato, sliced
A stoned (pitted) olive, halved (optional)

1 Put the bagel halves on a plate. Spread the cut sides with the tomato purée, then sprinkle with the oregano. Top with the cheese, then the tomato slices. Garnish each half with half an olive, if you like.

2 Microwave on High (100 per cent power) for about 1 minute or until the cheese melts and bubbles. Serve straight away.

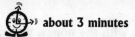 about 3 minutes

QUARTER-POUNDER WITH CHEESE

If you buy a better-quality burger, you'll get a better flavour – and it will contain more meat!

Serves 1

1 frozen quarter-pounder beefburger
1 round soft bread roll
Tomato ketchup (catsup)
Mayonnaise
2 thin slices cut from an unpeeled onion
A handful of shredded lettuce
1 Cheddar or processed cheese slice

1 Put the frozen beefburger on an upturned saucer or small plate standing on a larger plate (to let the fat run off). Cover with an inverted bowl.

2 Microwave on High (100 per cent power) for 1–2 minutes or until just cooked through, turning once half-way through. Do not overcook or the edges will go leathery.

3 Leave the burger to stand while you split the roll and spread a little ketchup and mayonnaise inside.

4 Separate the onion slices into rings, discarding the brown outer one and the first white layer.

5 Place the burger in the roll and top with the onion rings, then the lettuce, then the cheese slice. Top with the other half of the roll. Place on a serving plate.

6 Microwave for 20–30 seconds until the cheese is melting. Serve straight away.

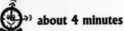 about 4 minutes

HOT BLT

You can vary this easy recipe with pretty much anything that takes your fancy – and just change the initials to match!

Serves 1

2 rashers (slices) of back bacon, rinded
2 slices of bread
Butter or margarine
2 tsp mayonnaise
1 tomato, sliced
1–2 crisp lettuce leaves

1 Lay the bacon rashers side by side on a plate, with kitchen paper (paper towel) underneath if you like your bacon crispy. Cover with a sheet of kitchen paper.

2 Microwave on High (100 per cent power) for 1½–2 minutes until cooked to your liking. As soon as it is cooked, take it off the kitchen paper or it will stick.

3 Meanwhile, spread the bread with butter or margarine, then spread one slice with the mayonnaise and top with the tomato slices and lettuce.

4 Lay the bacon on top and cover with the other slice of bread. Return to the microwave and cook for 20 seconds. Serve cut in half, if preferred.

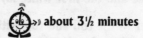 about 3½ minutes

HOT BEEF WRAP

**Keep flour tortillas in the freezer in their wrapper. Take the
pack out just long enough to loosen and remove one (or two).**

Serves 1

2 handfuls of frozen minced (ground) beef
1 tbsp tomato purée (paste)
1 tsp dried minced onion
¼ tsp dried oregano
¼ tsp chilli powder
½ tsp sugar
Salt and pepper
1 large or 2 small flour tortilla wraps
A small handful of grated Cheddar cheese
A handful of shredded lettuce

1 Put the minced beef in a small bowl and microwave on
High (100 per cent power) for 2 minutes, stirring twice,
until the grains are separate and no longer pink.

2 Stir in the tomato purée, minced onion, oregano, chilli
powder, sugar and some salt and pepper. Cover with a
plate. Microwave on High for 1 minute, stirring once.

3 Spread over half the tortilla(s) and top with cheese and
lettuce. Fold the uncovered side over the filling, then
fold in half again to a cone shape and serve.

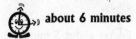 about 6 minutes

MELTED GOATS' CHEESE CRUMPETS WITH CRANBERRY RELISH

Crumpets are extremely cheap and a great source of complex carbohydrates for sustained energy.

Serves 1

1 tomato, chopped
2.5 cm/1 in piece of cucumber, chopped
1 tbsp cranberry sauce
1 tsp vinegar
2 crumpets
A small knob of butter or margarine
1 × 70 g/3 oz disc of goats' cheese

1 Mix the tomato with the cucumber, cranberry and vinegar. Chill until ready to serve.

2 Spread the crumpets with a scraping of butter or margarine and place on a plate. Microwave on Medium (50 per cent power) for 40 seconds or until the butter melts.

3 Cut the goats' cheese disc in half widthways and place one on top of each crumpet. Microwave on Medium for 1 minute until the cheese is just beginning to melt. Spread out slightly, then spoon the cold relish on top and eat straight away.

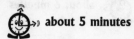 about 5 minutes

HOT COARSE HUMMUS WITH PITTA BREADS

This is a simple, substantial version of the popular smooth Greek dip. You can also pack it into warm pitta breads.

Serves 1

½ × 425 g/15 oz/large can of chick peas (garbanzos), drained
1 small garlic clove, crushed, or ½ tsp garlic purée (paste)
2 tbsp olive oil
2 tsp bottled lemon juice
Salt and pepper
2 pitta breads
A handful of olives

1 Put the chick peas in a bowl and crush thoroughly with a fork or a potato masher.

2 Add the garlic, oil and lemon juice and stir well.

3 Microwave on High (100 per cent power) for 1½ minutes. Remove from the oven and mix together vigorously with a fork. Season to taste and cover with a plate to keep warm.

4 Wrap the pitta breads in kitchen paper (paper towels) and microwave on High for 20 seconds. Cut into strips and serve with the hot hummus and some olives.

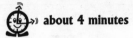 »» about 4 minutes

JACKET POTATO WITH SAVOURY TOPPINGS

If you use half a can of any of the suggested ingredients, store the remainder in the fridge for up to 3 days.

Serves 1

1 large potato, scrubbed

A small knob of butter or margarine

Hot Cheese and Bean

1 × 225 g/8 oz/small can of baked beans (or ½ a large can)

A handful of grated cheese

1 tsp brown table sauce (optional)

Hot Creamy Mushroom

3 mushrooms, chopped

2 tbsp crème fraîche

A pinch of dried oregano

Salt and pepper

Cool Tuna Mayo

½ × 185 g/6½ oz/small can of tuna, drained

2.5 cm/1 in piece of cucumber, diced

1 tbsp mayonnaise

A few drops of Worcestershire sauce (optional)

Pepper

Chilled Prawns in Thousand Island Dressing

1 tbsp mayonnaise
1 tsp tomato ketchup (catsup)
A dash of Worcestershire sauce or brown table sauce
A dash of bottled lemon juice
A good handful of frozen cooked, peeled prawns (shrimp), thawed

1 Prick the potato all over with a fork. Wrap in a piece of kitchen paper (paper towel). Microwave on High (100 per cent power) for about 4 minutes or until soft when squeezed, turning over once during cooking. Remove from the oven and leave to stand for 5 minutes while making the filling.

2 Mix together the ingredients for your chosen filling.

3 Unwrap the potato and place in a bowl. Cut a cross in the top of it and squeeze gently to open it up a bit. Add the butter or margarine.

4 Spoon the filling in and over the potato. For Hot Cheese and Bean or Hot Creamy Mushroom, return to the microwave and cook on High for about 1 minute until sizzling hot. Serve the other two as cold toppings. Eat straight away.

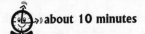about 10 minutes

CURRY CRUSTS AND VEGGIES WITH HOT PEANUT DUNK

**You don't have to use the veggies suggested here.
Experiment with other raw varieties.**

Serves 1–2

A knob of butter or margarine
1 garlic clove, crushed, or 1 tsp garlic purée (paste)
¼ tsp curry paste (or powder, but it's not quite as good)
1 thick crust from the end of a sliced loaf
2 tbsp peanut butter
3 tbsp water
1 tbsp soy sauce
1 tbsp clear honey
2 tsp bottled lemon juice
¼ tsp chilli powder or hot chilli sauce
1 green (bell) pepper, cut into strips
1 carrot, cut into strips
5 cm/2 in piece cucumber, cut into strips

1 Mash the butter or margarine with half the garlic and the curry paste. Spread on the crust of bread. Place on a sheet of kitchen paper (paper towel).

2 Put the remaining garlic in a small bowl with the remaining ingredients except the vegetables. Microwave on High (100 per cent power) for 1 minute. Stir until it looks curdled. Microwave for a further 1 minute and stir until thick and smooth.

3 Remove from the oven, cover and leave to stand while you microwave the bread on Medium (50 per cent power) for 20 seconds until the butter has melted. Remove from the oven and allow the butter to soak into the bread for a few seconds.

4 Cut the bread into large cubes and serve with the veggies to dip into the hot dunk.

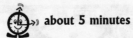 about 5 minutes

MICRO-TOASTED HAM AND CHEESE SANDWICH

Ring the changes with sliced tomato and cheese or sliced pickled onions and cheese for quick, easy snacks.

Serves 1

2 slices of bread
Butter or margarine
A scraping of English mustard (optional)
1 slice of ham
3 thin slices of Cheddar cheese

1 Toast the bread in a toaster or bake the slices in the microwave on a sheet of kitchen paper (paper towel) on High (100 per cent power) for 3–3½ minutes until crisp. Spread with a little butter or margarine.

2 Put one slice on a plate, buttered-side down. Add the mustard, then the ham, then the cheese. Top with the other slice of toast, buttered-side up. Microwave on High for about 40–60 seconds until the cheese is melting. Cut in half and serve.

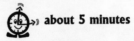 about 5 minutes

MEAT AND POULTRY MAIN MEALS

FEED ME

Chicken is probably one of my favourite things to cook in the microwave – it always comes out moist, tender and delicious. But any of the recipes in this chapter will give you a tasty, nutritious, innovative meal that won't break the bank but will fill you up and satisfy even the laziest and hungriest cook! They all have either built-in accompaniments or simple serving suggestions to give you all-round goodness.

CHICKEN CHOW MEIN

Look out for packs of fresh stir-fry veggies that are reduced for quick sale, then use them instead on the same day.

Serves 1

1 block of Chinese egg noodles
2 tsp sunflower oil
1 small skinless chicken breast, cut into dice
1 mug frozen stir-fry vegetables
1 small garlic clove, crushed, or ½ tsp garlic purée (paste)
½ tsp clear honey
1 tbsp soy sauce
½ tsp ground ginger

1 **Put the noodles in a fairly large bowl. Cover with water and microwave on High (100 per cent power) for 5 minutes, stirring twice, until soft. Leave to stand while you cook the chicken and vegetables.**

2 **Put the oil in a large bowl, add the chicken and microwave on High for 1 minute, stirring once.**

3 **Add the vegetables and garlic, stir well and microwave on High for 3 minutes, stirring once.**

4 **Add the honey, soy sauce and ginger and stir well. Drain the noodles and add to the chicken mixture. Stir well to mix, then microwave for 1 minute until piping hot.**

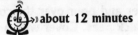

≫ about 12 minutes

CHICK PEA COUSCOUS WITH SWEET SPICED LAMB

Store the rest of the chick peas in a covered container in the fridge for up to three days (you could use them for the Hot Coarse Hummus recipe on page 71). Eat the remaining mandarins for dessert.

Serves 1

½ mug couscous
1 lamb or chicken stock cube
1 mug boiling water
½ × 425 g/15 oz/large can of chick peas (garbanzos), drained
1 mug minced (ground) lamb
1 small onion, finely chopped
1 small garlic clove, crushed, or ½ tsp garlic purée (paste)
2 tsp sunflower or olive oil
2 mushrooms, sliced
½ × 300 g/11 oz/medium can of broken mandarin segments
¼ tsp ground cumin
¼ tsp ground cinnamon
2 tsp tomato purée (paste)
Salt and pepper

1 Put the couscous in a bowl. Stir half the stock cube into the boiling water and pour over the couscous. Stir well, then add the chick peas. Cover with a plate.

2 Microwave on High (100 per cent power) for 5 minutes. Remove from the microwave, stir well with a fork to fluff up, then re-cover and leave to stand while cooking the lamb.

3 Mix together the lamb, onion, garlic, oil and mushrooms in a dish. Cover with a lid or plate and microwave on High for 2–3 minutes, stirring once or twice, until the grains of meat are no longer pink.

4 Blend the remaining stock cube with 4 tbsp boiling water. Add to the lamb mixture with the mandarins and their juice, the cumin, cinnamon, tomato purée and a sprinkling of pepper. Stir well and microwave uncovered on High for 5–6 minutes until cooked and tender. Taste and season with salt, if necessary.

5 Loosen the grains of couscous with a fork. Tip it on to a plate and spoon the lamb over.

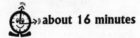

about 16 minutes

CHICKEN WITH PESTO

Pesto is useful to have in the fridge. You can stir a spoonful into cooked spaghetti and top it with grated cheese.

Serves 1

1 tbsp water
1 tsp cornflour (cornstarch)
1 tbsp pesto sauce from a jar
1 tbsp white wine, cider or apple juice
1 tsp bottled lemon juice
Salt and pepper
2 chicken thighs
1 mug pasta shapes
3 mugs water
To serve
A mixed salad

1 Mix together the 1 tbsp of water and cornflour in a small, shallow dish. Stir in the pesto, wine, cider or apple juice, lemon juice and a little salt and pepper.

2 Trim any flaps of skin off the chicken. Add the chicken thighs to the pesto mixture and turn them over to coat completely. If time, cover and leave to marinate in the fridge for 30 minutes – or even overnight.

3 Just before you cook the chicken, put the pasta in a bowl and add the 3 mugfuls of water. Microwave on High (100 per cent power) for 6–8 minutes just tender, stirring twice. Cover and leave to stand while you cook the chicken.

4 Cover the dish of chicken with a lid or plate and microwave on High for 3 minutes. Turn the chicken over, re-cover and cook for a further 3–5 minutes or until the chicken is tender, pulls away easily from the bones and the juices run clear, not pink, when pierced. Leave to stand for 3 minutes. Meanwhile, reheat the pasta for 1 minute, stir well, then drain in a colander.

5 Spoon the pasta on to a plate, add the chicken and all the sauce and serve with a mixed salad.

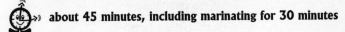 about 45 minutes, including marinating for 30 minutes

ONE-BOWL CHILLI CON CARNE WITH TORTILLAS

Chilli con carne is good with rice or tacos too. You could buy large cans of tomatoes and beans, which are cheaper.

Serves 1

½ mug minced (ground) beef
1 small onion, chopped
¼ tsp chilli powder
¼ tsp ground cumin
¼ tsp dried oregano
1 tsp tomato purée (paste)
A good pinch of sugar, salt and pepper
1 × 225 g/8 oz/small can of chopped tomatoes
1 × 225 g/8 oz/small can of red kidney beans, drained
2 large or 4 small flour tortillas

To serve

Grated cheddar cheese, shredded lettuce, chopped tomato and chopped cucumber

1 Put the mince, onion, spices and oregano in a bowl and microwave on High (100 per cent power) for about 2 minutes, stirring twice, until the meat is no longer pink and all the grains are separate.

2 Stir in the remaining ingredients except the tortillas. Cover with a sheet of kitchen paper (paper towel) to prevent spluttering and cook in the Microwave on High for 6 minutes, stirring once or twice, until rich and thick.

3 Remove from the microwave and leave to stand while you put the tortillas on a plate and cover with kitchen paper. Microwave on High for 20–30 seconds until hot.

4 Spoon the chilli con carne into the tortillas, top with a little cheese, lettuce, tomato and cucumber, roll up and serve.

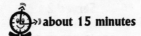 about 15 minutes

PORK AND GREENS STIR-FRY WITH BAMBOO SHOOTS AND RICE

This serves two to use all the bamboo shoots. If eating alone, cool half and store in the fridge for the next day.

Serves 2

½–1 mug long-grain rice
3–4 mugs boiling water
Salt
1 small head of spring (collard) greens
1 onion
1 tbsp sunflower oil
1 garlic clove, crushed, or 1 tsp garlic purée (paste)
1 pork shoulder steak, cut into thin strips
1 × 225 g/8 oz/small can of bamboo shoots, drained
2 tbsp soy sauce
2 tsp sugar
½ tsp chilli powder

1 Put the rice in a large bowl and add the boiling water. Microwave on High (100 per cent power) for 8–10 minutes, stirring once or twice, until the grains are just tender. Add a pinch of salt, then cover and leave to stand for 3 minutes. Check to see whether the grains are cooked to your liking, if not, cook a minute or two more. Drain well. Rinse with boiling water, if liked, and drain again.

2 Meanwhile, finely shred the greens, discarding any thick stump, and halve and slice the onion.

3 Put the oil in a large bowl. Add the onion, garlic and pork. Cover with a plate and microwave on High for 3 minutes, stirring twice.

4 Add the greens and bamboo shoots, stir well, re-cover and microwave on High for 2–3 minutes, stirring twice.

5 Add the soy sauce, sugar and chilli powder, stir well and microwave on High for 1 minute. If necessary, pop the rice back in the microwave for 30 seconds to reheat.

6 Spoon the rice into bowls, top with the pork mixture and serve.

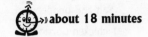 about 18 minutes

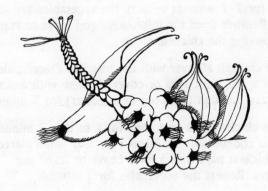

ROAST CHICKEN DINNER FOR ONE

It's sometimes nice to treat yourself to a meal that reminds you of home cooking!

Serves 1

1 potato, scrubbed and thinly sliced
1 carrot, peeled and thinly sliced
A handful of frozen peas
½ mug vegetable or chicken stock, made with ½ stock cube
Salt and pepper
1 chicken portion
½ tsp paprika

1 Arrange the vegetables in thin layers in a dish. Pour the stock over and sprinkle with salt and pepper. Cover with a lid or plate and microwave on High (100 per cent power) for 7–9 minutes or until the vegetables are tender. Remove from the microwave and leave to stand while cooking the chicken.

2 Rub the chicken all over with the paprika. Place upside-down in a dish with a lid or cover the dish with a plate. Microwave on High (100 per cent power) for 3 minutes.

3 Turn the chicken over and cook for a further 3 minutes until it is cooked and the juices run clear when pierced in the thickest part with a fork. Leave to stand for 5 minutes. Reheat the vegetables for 1 minute.

4 Transfer the chicken and vegetables to a plate. Pour any chicken juices over and serve.

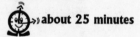 **»about 25 minutes**

CREAMY MUSHROOM CHICKEN WITH PASTA

Check the cooking time of the pasta on the packet. If it's the quick-cooking kind, it will take only 4–5 minutes.

Serves 1

½–1 mug small pasta shapes (depending on appetite)
A good handful of frozen peas or cut green beans
2–3 mugs boiling water
Salt and pepper
1 × 170 g/6 oz/small can of creamed mushrooms
1 tbsp milk
A pinch of dried thyme
1 skinless chicken breast, cut into chunks
A little dried parsley, to garnish

1 Put the pasta and peas or beans in a large dish and add the boiling water. Microwave on High (100 per cent power) for 6– 8 minutes or until almost tender. Add a pinch of salt, stir, re-cover and leave to stand.

2 Mix the creamed mushrooms with the milk and thyme in a separate dish. Add the chicken and make sure it is submerged in the sauce. Cover with a lid or plate and microwave on High for 3 minutes. Stir, re-cover and cook for a further 3 minutes until the chicken is cooked through. Taste and season, if necessary.

3 Check that the pasta is completely cooked (if not, return to the microwave for a minute or two). Drain in a colander, then stir into the chicken. Reheat on High for 1 minute, if necessary, until piping hot. Sprinkle with dried parsley and serve.

 about 18 minutes

GOULASH WITH QUICK GARLIC BREAD

As I keep saying, it's cheaper to buy a large can of chopped tomatoes, then use the rest for another recipe.

Serves 1

For the goulash

2 tsp sunflower oil

---

1 small onion, peeled and chopped

---

1 carrot, peeled and chopped

---

1 potato, diced

½ mug minced (ground) lamb or beef

---

1 tsp paprika

---

1 × 225 g/8 oz/small can of chopped tomatoes

---

1 tsp tomato purée (paste)

¼ tsp sugar

Salt and pepper

---

1 tbsp plain yoghurt or crème fraîche

For the garlic bread

1 thick slice of bread

A knob of butter or margarine

---

1 small garlic clove, crushed, or ½ tsp garlic purée (paste)

A pinch of dried mixed herbs (optional)

To serve

A green salad

---

1 To make the goulash, put the oil, onion, carrot, potato and meat in a dish. Cover with a lid or a plate. Microwave on High (100 per cent power) for 2 minutes, stirring once, until the grains of meat are separate and no longer pink.

2 Add the remaining goulash ingredients except the yoghurt or crème fraîche. Stir well. Cover and microwave on High for 10 minutes until everything is cooked and bathed in a rich sauce. Leave to stand while you prepare the garlic bread.

3 Put the bread on a plate. Mash the butter or margarine with the garlic and herbs, if using. Spread over the bread. Microwave on Medium (50 per cent power) for 20 seconds until the butter melts. Cut into quarters.

4 Spoon the yoghurt or crème fraîche on top of the goulash and serve with the garlic bread and a green salad.

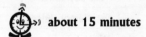 about 15 minutes

MINUTE STEAK WITH SPICY JUS AND CARROT JACKET POTATO

Thin frying steaks are not expensive and beating them helps to make them tender. Don't overcook, though!

Serves 1

1 large potato, scrubbed
1 carrot, peeled and grated
2 good knobs of butter or margarine
Salt and pepper
A pinch of ground cumin or cinnamon
1 spring onion (scallion), finely chopped
1 thin frying steak
1 tsp soy sauce
1 tbsp lemon juice
1 tbsp Worcestershire sauce
1 tsp fresh chopped or dried parsley

1 Prick the potato all over with a fork. Wrap in a piece of kitchen paper (paper towel) and microwave on High (100 per cent power) for 4–5 minutes or until soft when squeezed. Remove from the microwave.

2 Cut the potato in half and scoop out most of the potato into a bowl. Add the grated carrot. Mash together thoroughly with 1 knob of the butter or margarine and season with salt, pepper and the cumin or cinnamon. Pile back into the potato skins and put them on a plate.

3 Put the remaining knob of butter or margarine in a shallow dish. Add the spring onion and microwave on High for 1 minute.

4 Put the steak in a plastic bag and beat with a rolling pin or a bottle to tenderise it and flatten it even more. Smear the steak with the soy sauce.

5 Add the lemon juice, Worcestershire sauce, parsley and a sprinkling of salt and pepper to the spring onions, then add the steak and turn over in the sauce. Microwave on High for 1 minute. Remove from the oven and leave to stand while reheating the potato.

6 Put the potato on its plate back in the microwave and microwave for 1 minute. Add the steak and the juices to the plate and serve.

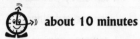 about 10 minutes

KEEMA CURRY ON NAAN

This curry can be served with rice (see page 23) or spooned into a large jacket potato (see page 23).

Serves 1

2 tsp sunflower oil
1 small onion, chopped
1 small garlic clove, crushed, or ½ tsp garlic purée (paste)
½ mug minced (ground) beef
2 tsp curry powder
¼ tsp ground ginger
1 tomato, chopped
5 tbsp water
A handful of frozen peas
Salt and pepper
1 large naan bread
To serve
A large salad

1 Put the oil in a largish bowl. Add the onion, garlic and mince and microwave on High (100 per cent power) for about 2 minutes, stirring once or twice, until the meat is no longer pink and all the grains are separate.

2 Stir in the curry powder and ginger and microwave for 30 seconds.

3 Add the remaining ingredients except the salt and pepper and naan. Microwave on High for 5 minutes, stirring twice. Remove from the microwave, season to taste, cover and leave to stand for 3 minutes.

4 Put the naan on a large plate. Cover with a piece of kitchen paper (paper towel) and microwave on High for 20 seconds. Spoon the curry on top and serve with a large salad.

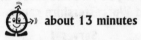 about 13 minutes

FAST PASTA BAKE WITH TOMATOES

If you aren't keen on salad, add a drained can of carrots or green beans to the pasta and heat for an extra 1 minute.

Serves 1

1 mug pasta shapes
1 × 225 g/8 oz/small can of minced (ground) steak with onions
A good pinch of dried mixed herbs
A good handful of grated Cheddar cheese
1 tomato, sliced
To serve
A green salad

1 Put the pasta in a bowl and cover with boiling water. Microwave on High (100 per cent power) for about 8–10 minutes or until tender. Leave to stand for 2 minutes, then drain and return to the bowl.

2 Stir in the meat and herbs and microwave on High for 1 minute, stirring once. Sprinkle the cheese over the surface and arrange the tomato slices around the edge. Microwave on High for about 1 minute or until the cheese has melted. Serve with a green salad.

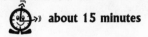 about 15 minutes

PORK AND VEGETABLE STROGANOFF

This will serve two if you just add more mushrooms, a little extra yoghurt and Worcestershire sauce, and extra pasta.

Serves 1

4 tagliatelle nests
Salt and pepper
1 tbsp sunflower oil
1 onion, halved and sliced
½ green or yellow (bell) pepper, sliced
1 pork shoulder steak, cut into thin strips
4 button mushrooms, sliced
1 courgette (zucchini), sliced
2 tsp cornflour (cornstarch)
½ mug plain yoghurt or crème fraîche
2 tsp Worcestershire sauce
A little chopped fresh or dried parsley

1 Put the tagliatelle nests in a large bowl. Cover with boiling water and add a pinch of salt. Microwave on High (100 per cent power) for about 6–8 minutes, stirring twice, until just cooked. Leave to stand while you cook the stroganoff.

2 Put the oil in a separate bowl with the onion and sliced pepper. Microwave on High for 2 minutes, stirring once.

3 Add the pork, mushrooms and courgette and stir well. Cover and microwave on High for 5 minutes, stirring twice.

4 Stir in the cornflour, yoghurt or crème fraîche and Worcestershire sauce. Microwave on High for 2 minutes, stirring twice. Season to taste.

5 Drain the pasta and tip on to a plate. Spoon the stroganoff on top and sprinkle with parsley.

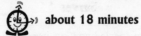 about 18 minutes

EASY CORN AND SPICED MINCE TACOS

Want a quick meal with lots of flavour? This is ideal for lunch, supper, or even after the pub!

Serves 1

1 × 225 g/8 oz/small can of minced (ground) steak with onions
¼ tsp chilli powder
1 tbsp tomato ketchup (catsup)
1 × 200 g/7 oz/small can of sweetcorn, drained
4 crispy tacos
4 lettuce leaves
A good handful of grated Cheddar cheese

1 Mix the steak with the chilli powder, ketchup and sweetcorn in a bowl. Microwave on High (100 per cent power) for 2–3 minutes, stirring twice, until piping hot. Remove from the microwave.

2 Separate the tacos and microwave on High for 1 minute.

3 Line each taco with a lettuce leaf, spoon in the chilli mixture and top with the cheese.

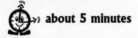 about 5 minutes

BRAISED LIVER WITH PEAS ON SWEDE MASH

Liver is great brain food as it's high in iron so it's good to make it part of your diet. Try parsnip instead of swede too.

Serves 1

1 potato, peeled and cut into small pieces
½ small swede (rutabaga), peeled and cut into small chunks
Salt and pepper
2 good knobs of butter or margarine
2 tsp plain (all-purpose) flour
½ mug water
½ beef stock cube
A good pinch of dried mixed herbs
3 slices of lamb's liver
A good handful of frozen peas

1 Put the potato and swede in a dish. Spread out and add enough water to just cover the vegetables. Cover with a lid or plate and microwave on High (100 per cent power) for about 9 minutes or until really tender, stirring twice. Add a sprinkling of salt and leave to stand while you cook the liver.

2 Put 1 knob of the butter or margarine in a shallow dish. Cover with a plate and microwave on High for 20 seconds until melted. Stir in the flour, then blend in the water until smooth. Crumble in the stock cube and add the herbs. Microwave on High for 2 minutes, stirring twice, until thickened.

3 Add the liver and peas and make sure the liver is covered by the gravy. Cover and microwave on High for 3 minutes until just cooked and the gravy is thick. Season to taste.

4 Pop the potato and swede back in the microwave and cook on High for 1 minute. Drain off the water. Add the remaining knob of butter and mash well with a potato masher or fork. Pile on a plate, add the liver and pea gravy and serve.

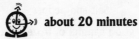 about 20 minutes

TURKEY STEAK WITH NOODLES AND TOMATO AND BASIL SAUCE

To use the remaining soup for a hearty snack, mix with canned tomatoes, microwave until hot and add grated cheese.

Serves 1

4 tagliatelle nests
Salt and pepper
A good handful of frozen peas
1 turkey breast steak
½ × 300 g/11 oz/medium can of cream of tomato soup
¼ tsp dried basil

1 Put the tagliatelle in a large bowl and cover with boiling water. Add a pinch of salt. Microwave on High (100 per cent power) for 5 minutes, stirring once. Stir again, add the peas and microwave on High for about 3 minutes until the tagliatelle is just cooked. Leave to stand while you cook the turkey.

2 Put the turkey steak in a shallow dish. Pour the soup over and add the basil and a sprinkling of salt and pepper. Microwave on High for 3 minutes until the turkey is tender and cooked through.

3 Drain the noodles. Put on a plate and top with the turkey and sauce.

>» about 14 minutes

HAM WITH PINEAPPLE, TOMATO AND CHEESE ON SCALLOPED POTATOES

Some ham steaks are small and round, others are larger and semi-circular. Use the rest of the pineapple for dessert.

Serves 1

A knob of butter or margarine
1 potato, scrubbed and sliced
4 tbsp milk
Salt and pepper
1 vacuum-packed ham steak
1 tomato, sliced
1 canned pineapple slice, cut into small pieces
1 Cheddar or Leerdammer cheese slice
To serve
A green salad

1 Smear a fairly shallow dish with the butter or margarine. Lay the potato slices in the dish, slightly overlapping if necessary but in a single layer. Pour the milk over. Season lightly with salt and pepper. Cover the dish with a plate and microwave on High (100 per cent power) for 5 minutes until the potatoes are almost tender.

2 Put the ham steak on top and microwave on High for a further 2 minutes. Top with the tomato, then the pineapple, then the cheese. Microwave for a further 2 minutes until the cheese melts and bubbles. Serve straight from the dish with a green salad.

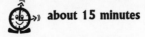 about 15 minutes

SPAGHETTI WITH MEATBALLS

You can shape the same mince mixture into a large flat burger, cook as the first part of step 3 and serve in a bun.

Serves 1

A small handful of spaghetti
Salt and pepper
½ mug minced (ground) beef
½ slice of bread, pulled into tiny pieces
1 tsp minced dried onion
¼ tsp dried oregano
1 tbsp grated Parmesan cheese, plus extra for sprinkling
2 tbsp water
1 × 225 g/8 oz/small can of chopped tomatoes
2 tsp tomato purée (paste)
½ tsp sugar
To serve
A green salad

1 Break the spaghetti into lengths to fit a shallow dish and spread out in the dish. Cover with plenty of boiling water. Microwave on High (100 per cent power) for about 8 minutes, stirring twice, until almost tender. Add a pinch of salt, cover and leave to stand while cooking the meatballs.

2 Mix the beef with the bread, onion, half the oregano, the Parmesan, water and a sprinkling of salt and pepper.

3 Shape the mixture into six small balls. Place in a second shallow dish. Lay a sheet of kitchen paper (paper towel) over the dish and microwave on High for 2 minutes, turning once. Lift out of the dish.

4 Mix the tomatoes with the purée, sugar, a little salt and pepper and the remaining oregano in the dish. Return the meatballs and turn over in the sauce. Microwave on High for 1–2 minutes or until the sauce is bubbling.

5 Drain the spaghetti and place in a bowl. Top with the meatballs and sauce and sprinkle with extra Parmesan. Serve with a green salad.

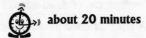 about 20 minutes

ALL-IN-ONE COTTAGE PIE

This is all cooked and served in one dish so there is very little washing up. It's a complete meal too.

Serves 1

1 small onion, chopped
½ mug minced (ground) beef
2 tsp plain (all-purpose) flour
½ beef stock cube
½ mug boiling water
1 × 300 g/11 oz/medium can of diced mixed vegetables, drained
A pinch of dried mixed herbs
Salt and pepper
1 potato, scrubbed or peeled and thinly sliced
A knob of butter or margarine

1 Put the onion and beef in a smallish dish that will hold at least 2 mugfuls of water. Microwave on High (100 per cent power) for 2 minutes, stirring once or twice, until the meat is no longer pink and all the grains are separate.

2 Stir in the flour. Blend the stock cube with the water, then stir into the meat. Microwave on High for 2 minutes until thickened. Stir in the vegetables and the herbs. Season to taste.

3 Lay the potato slices on top of the meat in a single layer, slightly overlapping if necessary. Sprinkle with a little salt and pepper and put little flakes of the butter or margarine all over the surface.

4 Cover with a plate and microwave on High for
10 minutes or until the potatoes are tender. If liked, put
the dish under a preheated grill (broiler) for about 5
minutes to brown the surface (but this isn't absolutely
necessary).

 about 20 minutes (25 minutes if you brown the top)

QUICK CASSOULET

This is nutritious and very tasty. You can ring the changes
with pieces of ham instead of bacon.

Serves 1

2 thick sausages, cut into chunks
1 rasher (slice) of bacon, rinded and diced
1 peperami stick, cut into chunks
1 × 400 g/14 oz/large can of baked beans
A pinch of dried mixed herbs
1 Weetabix or a handful of cornflakes or bran flakes
A handful of grated Cheddar cheese
To serve
Crusty bread and a mixed salad

1 Spread out the sausage and bacon pieces in a shallow
dish. Cover with kitchen paper (paper towel) and
microwave on High (100 per cent power) for 2 minutes.

2 Stir in the peperami chunks, the beans and herbs.
Microwave on High for 3 minutes until piping hot.

3 Crumble the Weetabix or flakes and mix with the cheese.
Scatter over the top of the cassoulet and microwave for
1 minute until the cheese melts. Serve with crusty bread.

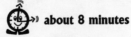 about 8 minutes

MEXICAN CHICKEN AND RICE POT

You can adjust the spices to suit your own taste. It's safer to err on the side of caution the first time.

Serves 1

2 tsp olive oil
1 small onion, chopped
1 small red (bell) pepper, chopped
1 rasher (slice) of smoked streaky bacon, diced
A small handful of frozen peas
¼ mug long-grain rice
¼ tsp ground turmeric
A good pinch of chilli powder
⅓ mug boiling water
½ chicken stock cube
2 chicken thighs
1 tsp paprika
1 bay leaf
Salt and pepper

1 Put the oil in a shallow dish. Add the onion, chopped pepper and bacon and microwave on High (100 per cent power) for 2 minutes, stirring twice.

2 Stir in the peas and rice until all the grains of rice are glistening. Add the turmeric, chilli powder, boiling water and stock cube and stir until the cube dissolves.

3 Trim any flaps of skin off the chicken, then dust the chicken all over with the paprika. Lay on top of the rice and tuck in the bay leaf. Sprinkle lightly with salt and pepper. Cover with a plate and microwave on High for 3 minutes.

4 Microwave for a further 15 minutes on Medium (50 per cent power) until the chicken is cooked through and the rice is tender and has absorbed nearly all the liquid. Leave to stand for 3 minutes, then remove the bay leaf and serve.

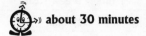 about 30 minutes

SAVOURY TURKEY STEAKWICH WITH TOMATO AND ONION SALAD

Ring the changes with different flavoured stuffings. The remaining stuffing will keep in the packet for ages.

Serves 1

1 turkey breast steak
1 tbsp milk
1 tsp soy sauce
85 g/3½ oz sage and onion stuffing mix
2 tbsp sunflower oil
2 tomatoes
1 small onion
1 tsp vinegar
A pinch of sugar, salt and pepper
1 large wholemeal roll (or 2 slices of bread)
Butter or margarine
1 tbsp mayonnaise
5 slices of cucumber
2 lettuce leaves

1 Put the turkey steak in a plastic bag and beat with a rolling pin or bottle to flatten.

2 Mix together the milk and soy sauce on a plate. Put the stuffing mix on another plate.

3 Dip the turkey in the milk mixture, then in the stuffing to coat completely.

4 Put half the oil in a shallow dish. Add the turkey steak, cover with a sheet of kitchen paper (paper towel) and microwave on High (100 per cent power) for 1 minute. Turn the turkey over and microwave for another 1 minute until cooked through. Remove from the microwave and leave to stand for 3 minutes.

5 Slice the tomatoes and arrange in a shallow bowl. Cut the onion into slices, peel off and discard the brown outer layer and the next layer and separate into rings. Lay the rings on top of the tomatoes. Trickle the remaining oil and the vinegar over, then sprinkle with the sugar, salt and pepper.

6 Split the roll and spread with a little butter or margarine. Spread one half with the mayonnaise. Lay the turkey in the roll and top with the cucumber and lettuce. Serve with the tomato and onion salad.

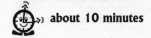 about 10 minutes

CHINESE PORK WITH SWEETCORN AND SESAME NOODLES

This is really easy to make but is a great oriental-style dish and very quick to put together.

Serves 1

A knob of butter or margarine
½ small green or red (bell) pepper, chopped
1 spring onion (scallion), chopped
1 small garlic clove, crushed, or ½ tsp garlic purée (paste)
1 tbsp cornflour (cornstarch)
1 tbsp vinegar
½ beef stock cube
½ mug boiling water
4 tsp soy sauce
1 tbsp golden (light corn) syrup
3 slices of belly pork, rind removed, cut into chunks
1 slab of Chinese egg noodles
1 × 200 g/7 oz/small can of sweetcorn
1 tbsp sesame seeds

1 Put the butter or margarine in a fairly large, shallow dish with the chopped pepper, onion and garlic. Microwave on High (100 per cent power) for 2 minutes, stirring once.

2 Stir in the cornflour, then the vinegar. Crumble the stock
cube into the boiling water and stir until dissolved.
Blend into the dish and add 3 tsp of the soy sauce and
the syrup. Microwave on High for 1 minute. Stir well
and microwave for a further 1 minute until thick.

3 Add the pork and turn each chunk to coat in the sauce.
Spread out, cover with a plate and microwave on
Medium-high (70 per cent power) for 15 minutes,
stirring twice. Cover and leave to stand for 5 minutes
while making the noodles.

4 Put the noodles in a bowl and pour boiling water over.
Stir and leave to stand for 5 minutes. Stir again, then
drain in a colander over the sink. Tip the noodles back
into the bowl and add the sweetcorn and the remaining
soy sauce.

5 Put the sesame seeds on a small plate. Put in the
microwave with the bowl of noodles and microwave on
High for 1 minute. Tip the seeds into the noodles. Lift
and stir with a spoon and fork to mix. Serve with the
pork.

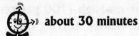 **about 30 minutes**

MACARONI FOR SUPPER

Pasta dishes are always a good standby and most people enjoy them. You could use other coloured peppers in the dish.

Serves 1

½ mug macaroni
2 mugs boiling water
Salt and pepper
A good knob of butter or margarine
1 green (bell) pepper, diced
1 small onion, chopped
1 slice of ham, diced
2 tsp cornflour (cornstarch)
½ mug milk
¼ tsp dried mixed herbs
A good handful of grated Cheddar cheese

1 Put the macaroni in a largish dish and add the boiling water. Microwave on High (100 per cent power) for 6–8 minutes until just tender, stirring once. Add a pinch of salt, cover and leave to stand.

2 Put the butter or margarine, diced pepper and onion in a bowl. Microwave on High for 2 minutes, stirring once or twice. Add the ham.

3 Stir in the cornflour, then the milk, stirring until no lumps of cornflour remain. Return to the microwave and cook on High for 2 minutes, stirring twice.

4 Stir in the herbs and cheese until melted. Drain the macaroni and stir into the sauce. Season to taste, then microwave on High for 1 minute. Serve from the dish.

≫ about 20 minutes

FISH MAIN MEALS

FEED ME

Fish is great brain food, quick to cook and delicious. Try to eat it twice a week and, as I don't recommend you keep making trips to the local chippie, why not try some of these simple and tasty recipes? Most use frozen or canned fish, so they can be made any time – as long as you keep a reasonably well-stocked cupboard and freezer!

COD STEAK WITH FAST MUSHROOM SAUCE ON VEGETABLE COUSCOUS

This filling and nutritious dish takes only a few minutes to prepare. Try other canned veggies in the couscous.

Serves 1

1 rectangular frozen cod steak
½ mug couscous
275 g/10 oz/medium can of diced mixed vegetables, drained
1 mug boiling water
½ chicken or vegetable stock cube
For the mushroom sauce
5 button mushrooms, sliced
A small knob of butter or margarine
1 tsp minced dried onion
A good pinch of dried mixed herbs
3 tbsp crème fraîche
Salt and pepper

1 Put the fish in a shallow dish. Cover with a plate or lid and microwave on High (100 per cent power) for 2 minutes. Remove from the microwave and leave to stand.

2 Put the couscous in a bowl with the vegetables. Blend the boiling water with the stock cube until dissolved, then pour into the bowl. Stir well. Cover with a plate and microwave on High for 4 minutes. Stir with a fork to fluff up and leave to stand while making the sauce.

3 Put the mushrooms, butter or margarine, dried onion and herbs in a small bowl. Microwave on High for 2 minutes, stirring once, until the mushrooms are soft. Stir in the crème fraîche and season to taste. Microwave on High for 1 minute.

4 Return the fish to the microwave and cook on High for 30–60 seconds until opaque. Pour any juices into the sauce.

5 Stir the couscous and spoon on to a plate. Top with the fish and spoon the sauce over.

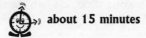 about 15 minutes

SEAFOOD LASAGNE

This is simply a dish thrown together from convenience foods. It will reheat perfectly the next day.

Serves 2–3 (depending on appetite)

1 × 400 g/14 oz/large can of chopped tomatoes
1 tbsp tomato purée (paste)
1 tsp Worcestershire sauce
1 × 185 g/6½ oz/small can of tuna, drained
6 seafood sticks, cut into chunks
6 mushrooms, sliced
1 tsp dried minced onion
½ tsp dried mixed herbs
Salt and pepper
6 sheets of lasagne
1 × 295 g/10½ oz/medium can of condensed mushroom or celery soup
½ can of milk
A good handful of grated Cheddar cheese
To serve
Crusty bread and a green salad

1 Mix the tomatoes with the tomato purée, then stir in the Worcestershire sauce, tuna, seafood sticks, mushrooms, dried onion, the herbs and a little salt and pepper.

2 Spread a thin layer of the fish mixture in a shallow rectangular dish, about 23 × 15 cm/9 × 6 in. Place two sheets of lasagne on top, breaking them to fit, if necessary.

3 Top with half the remaining fish mixture, then two more sheets of lasagne, then the remaining fish mixture, then the last of the lasagne.

4 Mix the soup with the milk and cheese and spoon over the top.

5 Microwave on High (100 per cent power) for 10–15 minutes until the pasta feels soft when you insert a knife down through the centre. The knife blade should also feel searingly hot when you take it out.

6 If liked, put the lasagne under a preheated grill (broiler) to brown the surface (but this is not absolutely necessary).

7 Serve with crusty bread and a green salad.

 about 25 minutes (30 minutes if you brown the top)

SALMON AND BROCCOLI BAKE

If you haven't got a huge appetite, this can be served cold the next day. Use the rest of the salmon for sarnis.

Serves 1–2

2 slices of bread
Butter or margarine
1 small head of broccoli, about 100 g/4 oz, broken into small florets
½ × 200 g/7 oz/small can of pink salmon, drained
A handful of grated Cheddar cheese
1 egg
¾ mug milk
Salt and pepper
4 tomatoes, sliced

1 Spread the bread with a little butter or margarine and use to line a shallow dish, a whole slice in the base, the other cut into strips to line the sides.

2 Put the broccoli in a separate dish and spread it out. Add 2 tbsp water. Cover with a lid or a plate and microwave on High (100 per cent power) for 3 minutes until almost tender. Leave to stand for 2 minutes, then lift out of the dish, retaining the cooking liquid, and place in the bread-lined dish.

3 Remove any dark skin from the salmon, separate the fish into chunks and place in the dish with the broccoli (including any bones as they are very good for you). Scatter the cheese over.

4 Beat the egg and milk into the broccoli water in the dish.
Season with a sprinkling of salt and pepper. Pour over
the fish and broccoli, making sure it soaks the bread
around the sides too.

5 Microwave on High for 6 minutes until nearly set.
Arrange the tomato slices over the surface, then
microwave for a further 8 minutes until the filling is set
and the tomatoes are just cooked. Serve straight from
the dish.

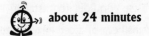 about 24 minutes

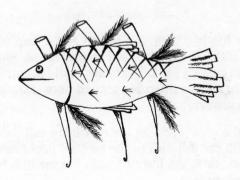

NO-EFFORT COD AND VEGETABLE PIE

You can make this with smoked fish or even a can of tuna to ring the changes. There is no need to cook tuna first.

Serves 1

1 rectangular frozen cod steak, thawed slightly and cut into cubes
5 tbsp milk
1 tsp cornflour (cornstarch)
1 × 200 g/7 oz/small can of diced mixed vegetables, drained
A good pinch of dried mixed herbs
Salt and pepper
1 portion of instant mashed potato
A knob of butter or margarine
A handful of grated Cheddar cheese
A small handful of cornflakes

1 Put the fish in a shallow dish and add 4 tbsp of the milk. Cover with a lid or plate and microwave on High (100 per cent power) for 2–3 minutes until just cooked through, stirring the cubes around once. Remove from the microwave.

2 Blend the cornflour with the remaining milk in a cup or mug. Tilt the fish dish so the cooking juices run to one side and stir in the blended milk. Put the dish back on the work surface.

3 Stir in the vegetables and the herbs. Taste and season. Microwave on High for 1 minute. Stir again.

4 Make up the mashed potato according to the packet directions, adding the butter or margarine. Pile on top of the fish mixture and sprinkle with the cheese, then crush the cornflakes over. Microwave on High for a further 1–2 minutes until the cheese has melted.

 about 10 minutes

TUNA FONDUE

This is a good meal to share with friends, but if you are eating alone make half and reheat the rest another day.

Serves 4

1 mug grated Cheddar cheese
1 small carton of single (light) cream
1 × 185 g/6½ oz/small can of tuna, drained
2 tbsp white wine, lager or apple juice
1 tsp paprika

To serve

Fingers of carrot, celery and cucumber, small tomatoes or radishes and cubes of French bread

1 Put all the ingredients in a bowl. Microwave on High (100 per cent power) for about 5 minutes, stirring every minute or so, until thick and the cheese has melted.

2 Serve the bowl of fondue with loads of veggies and bread to dip in.

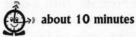 about 10 minutes

COD AND BACON KEBABS ON GARLIC BUTTER COUSCOUS

Make sure you use wooden skewers – if you use metal ones your microwave will arc, causing sparks and damage.

Serves 1

½ mug couscous
1 mug boiling water
Salt and pepper
1 tomato, quartered
1 rectangular frozen cod steak, cut into 8 cubes while still frozen
3 rashers (slices) of streaky bacon, rinded and halved
A good knob of butter or margarine
1 small garlic clove, crushed, or ½ tsp garlic purée (paste)
A small handful of chopped fresh parsley
To serve
A mixed salad

1 Put the couscous in a bowl. Add the boiling water and a sprinkling of salt and pepper and stir well. Cover with a plate. Microwave on High (100 per cent power) for 4 minutes, stirring twice. Remove from the microwave, stir with a fork to fluff up, re-cover and leave to stand while making the kebabs.

2 Thread a piece of tomato, then a cube of fish, then a piece of bacon, folded concertina fashion, on to a skewer. Add another piece of fish, then bacon, then fish, then bacon and finish with a piece of fish and finally a piece of tomato. Do the same with the second skewer.

3 Put the butter or margarine in a small bowl. Cover with a piece of kitchen paper (paper towel) and microwave on High for 20 seconds or until the fat has melted.

4 Smear a little over the kebabs (preferably with a pastry brush but otherwise use the back of a teaspoon). Lay the kebabs on a plate. Cover with a second plate or a lid and microwave on High for 3–4 minutes, turning once, until cooked through.

5 Meanwhile, stir the garlic into the remaining melted butter or margarine. Pour into the couscous with the parsley and stir well. Taste and re-season if necessary. Reheat in the microwave for 30 seconds, if necessary. Move the kebabs to one side of the plate and pile the couscous alongside. Serve with a mixed salad.

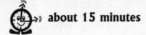 about 15 minutes

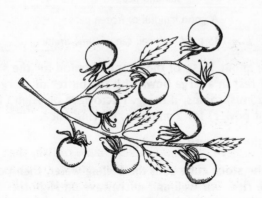

TUNA RISOTTO WITH TOMATO SALAD

You can make double the quantity, then reheat the rest of the risotto on a covered plate the next day.

Serves 1

1 small onion, chopped
A knob of butter or margarine
2 mushrooms, sliced (optional)
½ mug long-grain rice
½ chicken or vegetable stock cube
1 ¼ mugs boiling water
2 tomatoes
1 tbsp olive oil
1 tsp wine vinegar
A pinch of sugar
Salt and pepper
A good handful of frozen peas
½ × 185 g/6½ oz/small can of tuna, drained

1 Reserve about 1 tsp of the chopped onion for the salad. Put the rest in a large bowl with the butter or margarine and the mushrooms, if using. Microwave on High (100 per cent power) for 2 minutes, stirring once.

2 Stir in the rice until glistening.

3 Blend the stock cube with the boiling water, then pour into the rice. Stir well and microwave on High for 8 minutes, stirring every 2 minutes.

4 Meanwhile, slice the tomatoes and place in a small dish. Chop the reserved onion a bit more finely and scatter over. Trickle the oil and vinegar over and sprinkle with the sugar and a little salt and pepper. Toss gently with the hands and leave to stand for at least 5 minutes to allow the flavours to develop.

5 Add the peas and tuna to the risotto, stir again and microwave on High for 4 minutes or until the rice is just tender and has absorbed the liquid. Stir and season to taste with salt and pepper. Serve with the tomato salad.

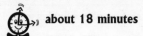 about 18 minutes

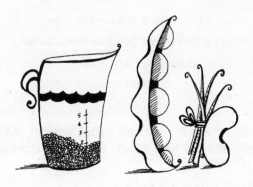

STARBURST SARDINE SCONE PIZZA

This is a soft pizza with a great flavour that would also serve two as a snack. Try other toppings, if you like.

Serves 1

½ mug plain (all-purpose) flour, plus extra for dusting
A pinch of salt
1 tsp baking powder
2 tbsp sunflower or olive oil, plus extra for greasing
1 egg, beaten
2 tbsp tomato purée (paste)
2 tbsp water
½ tsp dried oregano
1 tbsp soft cheese with chives (optional)
A good handful of grated Cheddar cheese
1 × 125 g/4½ oz/small can of sardines, drained
A few olives (optional)
To serve
A green salad

1 Mix the flour with the salt and baking powder. Add the oil and egg and mix with a fork, then with your hands, to form a soft dough.

2 Smear a dinner plate with a little oil. Put the dough on the plate and press out to a round about 18 cm/7 in diameter and about 5 mm/¼ in thick.

3 Cover with a sheet of kitchen paper (paper towel) and microwave on High (100 per cent power) for 1½ minutes.

4   Mix the tomato purée with the water and spread over the surface. Sprinkle with the oregano, then smear the soft cheese with chives, if using, on top. Sprinkle with the grated cheese. Arrange the sardines on top in a starburst pattern and scatter the olives around, if using.

5   Microwave on High for 2 minutes until the scone is cooked through and the cheese is melted and bubbling. Loosen the pizza with a knife or a fish slice, transfer to a plate and serve with a green salad.

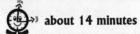 about 14 minutes

THAI-STYLE CRAB CAKES WITH SWEET CHILLI SAUCE

These cakes need firm handling. The mixture is quite wet so you need to squeeze it when you dip it in the crumbs.

Serves 1–2

A handful of long-grain rice
1 mug boiling water
1 red (bell) pepper, finely chopped
1 spring onion (scallion), finely chopped
1 slice of bread, crumbled into small pieces
8 seafood sticks
¼ tsp lemon juice
A good pinch of chilli powder
Salt and pepper
1 egg, beaten
4 tbsp bought dried breadcrumbs
½ tsp paprika
To serve
Sweet chilli sauce and a large salad

1 Put the rice in a fairly large bowl. Add the boiling water and microwave on High (100 per cent power) for 9 minutes.

2 Add the chopped pepper and the spring onion and microwave on High for 1 minute. Drain in a colander to remove any remaining water and tip the rice mixture back into the bowl. Add the crumbled bread to the rice. Mash the seafood sticks with a fork and add to the rice

with the lemon juice, chilli powder and a sprinkling of salt and pepper. Add the beaten egg and mix together to bind. The mixture will be wet.

3 Mix the dried breadcrumbs with the paprika on a plate. Shape the rice mixture into four cakes. Dip in the breadcrumbs, then squeeze to reshape and dip again until thoroughly coated. Reshape with the hands to form coated cakes. Chill for 30 minutes before cooking, if time.

4 Place the cakes around the edge of a plate. Cover with a sheet of kitchen paper (paper towel) and microwave on High for 3 minutes or until the cakes are set. Serve with sweet chilli sauce and a large salad.

 about 25 minutes, plus chilling time

COD WITH TOMATOES, OLIVES AND PEPPERS ON VEGETABLE RICE

We should all eat more fish and frozen cod steaks are a very good buy, but you can use any other white fish.

Serves 1

½ mug long-grain rice
½ chicken or vegetable stock cube
1¼ mugs boiling water
A handful of frozen peas
3 mushrooms, sliced
1 small onion, chopped
½ small green (bell) pepper, chopped
1 tbsp olive oil
1 small garlic clove, crushed, or ½ tsp garlic purée
5 tbsp passata (sieved tomatoes)
¼ tsp dried mixed herbs
2 tsp sliced stoned (pitted) black olives
¼ tsp sugar
1 rectangular frozen cod steak, cut into cubes
1 tbsp plain (all-purpose) flour
Salt and pepper

1 Put the rice in a large bowl. Stir the stock cube into the boiling water until dissolved, then stir into the rice. Microwave on High (100 per cent power) for 5 minutes, stirring twice.

2 Add the peas and mushrooms and microwave on High for 5 minutes until the rice is tender and has absorbed all the liquid. Remove from the microwave, cover and leave to stand.

3 Put the onion, chopped pepper and oil in a separate bowl and microwave on High for 2 minutes.

4 Add the remaining ingredients except the fish, flour and seasoning to the onion and pepper mixture. Microwave for 1 minute.

5 Mix the cod cubes with the flour and add to the tomato mixture. Microwave for 3 minutes, stirring once, until the fish is cooked. Season to taste. If necessary, pop the rice back in the microwave and cook for 1 minute to reheat. Pile on to a plate and top with the fish mixture.

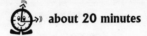 about 20 minutes

FILO CHEESY SALMON

Filo pastry can be frozen, thawed enough to remove the
sheets that you need, then rewrapped and frozen again.

Serves 1

1 sheet of filo pastry (paste)
1 potato, peeled and cut into small cubes
A handful of French (green) beans, cut into chunks (or frozen ones)
4 tbsp water
1 piece of salmon fillet (about 150 g/5 oz)
A pinch of salt
2 tbsp cheese spread
2 tbsp milk
To serve
1 tomato, sliced

1 Gently scrunch up the filo pastry so it looks like a
  crumpled sheet of paper. Place on a plate and microwave
  on High (100 per cent power) for 2 minutes until crisp.

2 Put the potato and beans in a bowl with the water.
  Cover with a plate and microwave on High for
  4–5 minutes until just cooked.

3 Spread the veggies out and lay the fish in the centre. Re-
  cover and microwave on High for 2–3 minutes until
  everything is cooked. Lift the fish out of the dish and cut
  it into pieces, removing the skin. Sprinkle the vegetables
  with the salt, stir, leave to stand for 1 minute, then
  drain in a colander, reserving the liquid, and set aside.

4 Add the cheese spread and milk to the reserved liquid.
  Cover with a lid or plate. Microwave on High for
  2 minutes, stirring twice with a fork or a wire whisk

until blended. Add the fish and vegetables and stir in gently. Microwave for 1 minute.

5 Spoon the fish mixture on to a plate and top with the crisp filo pastry. Serve with the tomato slices.

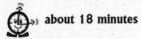 about 18 minutes

YELLOW FISH AND RICE

This is so simple to make but is really tasty, with the spring onion just adding that extra bite.

Serves 1

1 spring onion (scallion), trimmed and chopped
½ mug long-grain rice
A handful of sliced green beans
½ mug passata (sieved tomatoes)
¾ mug boiling water
¼ tsp dried basil
¼ tsp sugar
Salt and pepper
1 small piece of yellow smoked haddock, cod, or whiting fillet (about 150 g/5 oz)

1 Mix together everything except the fish in a dish. Cover with a lid or a plate. Microwave on High (100 per cent power) for 8 minutes until almost tender and most of the liquid has been absorbed.

2 Meanwhile, cube the fish, discarding the skin. Stir into the rice, re-cover and microwave on High for 4 minutes or until cooked. Leave to stand for 5 minutes before serving.

 about 20 minutes

PAELLA

This is a total cheat but the result tastes brilliant and it takes only minutes to put together and cook.

Serves 2

2 chicken thighs
½ tsp soy sauce
1 × 120 g/4½ oz packet of savoury vegetable rice
1½ mugs boiling water
¼ tsp dried oregano
A handful of frozen prawns (shrimp)
Salt and pepper
To serve
A mixed salad

1 Trim any flaps of skin off the chicken thighs. Smear the chicken with the soy sauce. Put the chicken in a shallow dish. Cover with a sheet of kitchen paper (paper towel) or a plate and microwave on High (100 per cent power) for 4 minutes.

2 Add the rice, water and oregano. Stir well. Microwave uncovered on High for 16 minutes, stirring twice.

3 Add the prawns and microwave for 2 minutes. Leave to stand for 2 minutes until everything is cooked and the rice has absorbed the liquid. If necessary, cook for 1–2 more minutes until the liquid has absorbed. Season to taste and serve with a mixed salad.

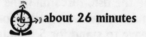 about 26 minutes

VEGETARIAN MAIN MEALS

FEED ME

You don't have to be a non-meat eater to enjoy these tasty and nutritious meals. They're often extremely cheap to make and will fill you up well. If you are a true vegetarian, make sure that the ingredients you use are suitable – everything from cheese to Worcestershire sauce needs to be clearly marked as okay for you to eat.

MUSHROOM QUICHE

For speed, put a bought cooked pastry case in a shallow dish, then continue from step 5.

Serves 1–2

¾ mug plain (all-purpose) flour, plus extra for dusting
3 tbsp soft butter or margarine
Salt and pepper
1–2 tsp cold water
6 mushrooms, sliced
1 small onion, peeled and sliced
½ tsp dried oregano
1 egg
½ mug milk
A good handful of grated Cheddar cheese

1 Put the flour in a bowl and add 2 tbsp of the butter or margarine and a pinch of salt. Mash with a fork until the mixture looks like crumbly lumps.

2 Mix in the water, a teaspoonful at a time, and mix to form a soft but not sticky dough.

3 Squeeze gently together into a ball, then press into an 18 cm/7 in shallow flan (pie) dish (or a similar dish) so it lines the base and sides evenly without any cracks.

4 Prick the base with a fork. Line the pastry (paste) with a sheet of kitchen paper (paper towel) and microwave on High (100 per cent power) for 3 minutes. Remove the paper and microwave for a further 1 minute until set. Remove from the oven.

5 Put the mushrooms, onion and the remaining margarine in a small bowl. Microwave on High for 2 minutes. Stir, then microwave for a further 1 minute. Tip into the pastry case and sprinkle with the oregano.

6 Break the egg into the mushroom bowl. Whisk in the milk and a little salt and pepper. Cover the mushroom mixture with the cheese, then pour in the egg and milk. Microwave on Medium (50 per cent power) for 15 minutes until set. Leave to stand for 5 minutes before serving.

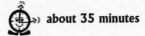 about 35 minutes

TOFU AND MUSHROOM CURRY

The rest of the tofu can be wrapped and kept in the fridge for several days.

Serves 1

½ mug long-grain rice
2–3 mugs boiling water
A pinch of salt
1 tbsp sunflower or olive oil
½ block of firm tofu, drained and cubed
1 tbsp milk
3 mushrooms, sliced
A knob of butter or margarine
1 heaped tsp Madras curry paste
1 tbsp peanut butter
5 tbsp water
1 tbsp raisins
To serve
Bottled lemon juice and a green salad

1 Put the rice in a bowl. Add the water. Stir, then microwave on High (100 per cent power) for 8–10 minutes until the rice is almost tender. Add the salt, cover and leave to stand while making the curry.

2 Put the oil in a shallow dish. Microwave on High for 20 seconds. Dip the tofu in the milk, arrange around the edges of the dish and turn over in the oil. Microwave on High for 3 minutes. Lift out of the dish.

3 Put the mushrooms and butter or margarine in the dish and microwave on High for 2 minutes.

4 Stir in the remaining ingredients until blended. Microwave on High for 1 minute. Add the tofu and microwave for a further 30 seconds.

5 Reheat the rice for 1 minute, if necessary. Stir and spoon on to a plate. Add the curry and serve with a sprinkling of lemon juice and a green salad.

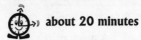 about 20 minutes

SWEETCORN AND BUTTER BEAN CONCHIGLIE WITH CHEESE

It's easier to make this for two people as that uses the full cans of ingredients.

Serves 2

1½–2 mugs conchiglie (pasta shells)
4 mugs of boiling water
A pinch of salt
1 × 200 g/7 oz/small can of sweetcorn, drained
425 g/15 oz/large can of butter (lima) beans, drained
1 × 300 g/11 oz/medium can of cream of mushroom soup (NOT condensed soup)
¼ tsp dried mixed herbs
1 small garlic clove, crushed, or ½ tsp garlic purée (paste)
A good handful of grated Cheddar cheese
A little dried parsley or paprika, to garnish
To serve
A green salad

1 Put the pasta in a large bowl and add the boiling water. Stir, then microwave on High (100 per cent power) for 8–10 minutes, stirring twice, until the pasta is just tender but still with some texture. Add the salt, then cover and leave to stand for 2 minutes.

2 Drain the pasta and return to the bowl. Stir in all the remaining ingredients. If you're not eating it all now, spoon half into a plastic container with a lid and store in the fridge.

3 Microwave on High for 2–3 minutes until piping hot, stirring gently twice.

4 Sprinkle with dried parsley or paprika and serve with a
   green salad.

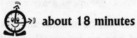 about 18 minutes

MIXED BEAN GOULASH

You could use a small can of chopped tomatoes instead of
the passata and then omit the water

Serves 1

1 small onion, chopped
½ small green (bell) pepper, chopped
2 tsp olive or sunflower oil
2 tsp paprika
3 tbsp passata (sieved tomatoes)
3 tbsp water
1 × 425 g/15 oz/large can of mixed pulses, drained
1 tsp caraway seeds (optional)
A pinch of sugar, salt and pepper
A spoonful of plain yoghurt, to garnish
To serve
Crusty bread and a green salad

1 Put the onion, chopped pepper and oil in a large bowl
   and microwave on High (100 per cent power) for
   2 minutes, stirring once.

2 Stir in all the remaining ingredients. Microwave on High
   for 5 minutes, stirring twice.

3 Ladle into a bowl, garnish with the yoghurt and serve
   with crusty bread and a green salad.

 about 10 minutes

MUSHROOM AND PEANUT PILAF

This sounds an unusual combination but give it a go as it really works and has an interesting mild spicy flavour.

Serves 1

2 tsp olive or sunflower oil
1 small onion, finely chopped
½ small green or yellow (bell) pepper, stalk and seeds removed, chopped
1 small garlic clove, crushed, or ½ tsp garlic purée (paste)
4 mushrooms, sliced
½ tsp garam masala
¼ tsp ground ginger
½ mug long-grain rice
½ vegetable stock cube
1¼ mugs boiling water
A handful of roasted peanuts
Salt and pepper

1 Put the oil, onion, chopped pepper, garlic, mushrooms, garam masala and ginger in a bowl. Stir to coat in the oil, then microwave on High (100 per cent power) for 2 minutes, stirring once.

2 Add the rice and stir until glistening with oil.

3 Stir the stock cube into the water until dissolved and add to the rice with the peanuts. Stir well, then microwave on Medium-high (70 per cent power) for about 15 minutes, stirring twice, until the rice is cooked and has absorbed the liquid.

4 Stir the rice and season with salt and pepper to taste. Leave to stand for 3 minutes before serving.

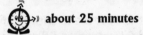 **about 25 minutes**

CHEESE-TOPPED POLENTA WITH RATATOUILLE

Packs of ready-made polenta are available with the pasta and Italian sauces in the supermarket.

Serves 1–2

½ slab of polenta, cut into slices about 7 mm/⅓ in thick
1 × 425 g/15 oz/large can of ratatouille
A good handful of grated Cheddar cheese
1 tbsp grated Parmesan cheese
2 tomatoes, sliced
A few chopped fresh basil leaves (optional)
To serve
Crusty bread and a green salad

1 Arrange the slabs of polenta in a starburst pattern in a shallow dish.

2 Spoon the ratatouille over so you can still see the tips of the polenta.

3 Sprinkle with the cheeses and arrange the tomato slices attractively on top.

4 Microwave on High (100 per cent power) for 3–4 minutes until the cheese has melted and everything is piping hot. Garnish with the chopped basil leaves, if using (they add flavour as well as look nice), and serve with crusty bread and a green salad.

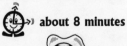 **about 8 minutes**

TABBOULEH WITH FETA AND OLIVES

This delicious salad is best made with fresh herbs to get the right colour and flavour.

Serves 1

½ mug bulghar (cracked wheat)
1½ mugs water
½ small garlic clove, crushed, or ½ tsp garlic purée (paste)
A small handful of chopped fresh parsley
A small handful of chopped fresh mint
1 tsp lemon juice
1 tbsp olive oil
Salt and pepper
2.5 cm/1 in piece of cucumber, finely chopped
1 tomato, chopped
¼ small block of Feta cheese, cut into cubes
6 black olives
To serve
Crusty bread

1 Put the bulghar in a bowl. Add the water, stir, cover with a lid or plate and microwave on High (100 per cent power) for 5 minutes, stirring twice. Leave to stand for 30 minutes. Drain, if necessary, then stir with a fork.

2 Add the garlic, herbs, lemon juice and oil and season lightly. Stir well. Stir in the cucumber and tomato and top with the cheese and olives. Serve with crusty bread.

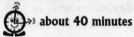 about 40 minutes

CAULIFLOWER CHEESE BAKE

Use the rest of the cauliflower florets to serve as dippers
for the Tuna Fondue (if you eat fish) on page 139.

Serves 1

½ small cauliflower, cut into small florets
2 slices of bread, buttered
A good handful of grated Cheddar cheese
1 egg
½ mug milk
Salt and pepper
1 tomato, sliced

1 Put the cauliflower in a shallow individual dish, arranged
with the heads towards the centre. Add 3 tbsp water,
cover with a lid or a small plate and microwave on High
(100 per cent power) for 3–4 minutes until tender.
Drain in a colander into the sink.

2 Wipe out the dish, then line with the bread, cutting it to
fit. Add the cauliflower and sprinkle with the cheese.

3 Break the egg into a small bowl or mug. Whisk in the
milk with a fork or a wire whisk. Season well, then pour
over the cheese so it coats the bread completely.
Arrange the tomato slices around the top.

4 Microwave on High for 2 minutes. Turn the setting to
Medium (50 per cent power) and cook for a further
6–8 minutes or until set. Leave to stand for 2 minutes,
then serve.

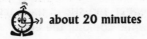 about 20 minutes

BARLEY RISOTTO WITH GARLIC MUSHROOMS AND EGGS

Pearl barley is a cheap alternative to rice and makes a delicious change. Try it with the addition of peppers.

Serves 1

½ mug pearl barley
1 small garlic clove, crushed, or ½ tsp garlic purée (paste)
2 small knobs of butter or margarine
1 vegetable stock cube
1¾ mugs boiling water
4 mushrooms, sliced
Salt and pepper
1 tbsp chopped fresh or 1 tsp dried parsley
2 eggs
To serve
Crusty bread and tomatoes

1 Put the barley, garlic and 1 knob of the butter or margarine in a bowl.

2 Blend the stock cube with the boiling water until dissolved and pour into the bowl. Stir, then microwave on High (100 per cent power) for 15 minutes.

3 Add the mushrooms, stir and microwave on High for 20–22 minutes until the barley is tender and the liquid has almost absorbed but the mixture is 'creamy'. Season with salt and pepper and stir in the parsley. Cover and leave to stand while cooking the eggs.

4 Smear two saucers or small plates with the remaining butter or margarine. Break an egg on to each and prick the yolks gently with a fork. Cover with a large plate or two small plates. Microwave on Medium-high (70 per cent power) for 1 minute. Leave to stand for 1 minute, then microwave on Medium-high for a further 1 minute or until the eggs are cooked to your liking.

5 Spoon the barley mixture into a large shallow bowl. Slide the eggs on top and serve with crusty bread and some tomatoes.

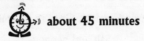 about 45 minutes

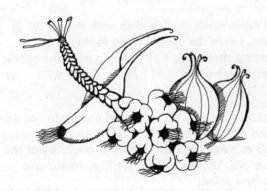

POTATOES BAKED WITH GARLIC AND CHEESE

For meat eaters, this is also delicious served as an accompaniment to everything from chops to sausages.

Serves 1

A small knob of butter or margarine
1 potato, scrubbed and thinly sliced
1 small garlic clove, crushed, or ½ tsp garlic purée (paste)
A good handful of grated Cheddar, Gruyère or Emmental (Swiss) cheese
Salt and pepper
1 egg
½ mug milk
To serve
A mixed salad

1 Smear a fairly small shallow dish with the butter or margarine. Layer the potato slices in the dish, interspersing them with tiny bits of garlic, the cheese and a sprinkling of salt and pepper. Finish with a layer of cheese.

2 Beat together the egg and milk and pour into the dish. Cover and microwave on High (100 per cent power) for about 10 minutes until the potato is cooked and the mixture is set. Leave to stand for 5 minutes, then serve with a mixed salad.

 about 20 minutes

SWEET THINGS

FEED ME

These are mostly snacky comfort foods for when you're studying late or need a cooking break when the words for your essay just won't come. A few are great desserts, all are sweet and delicious.

TREACLE SPONGE

Comfort food at its best. Serve it with canned custard and more syrup for decadence!

Serves 4

½ × 250 g/9 oz/small tub of soft margarine
3–4 tbsp golden (light corn) syrup
2 eggs
½ mug sugar
1 mug self-raising flour
1 tsp baking powder
2 tbsp water

1 Smear the inside of a pudding basin – or a narrow, deep dish that will hold 3 mugfuls of water – with a little of the margarine. Spoon the syrup into the base.

2 Put the remaining margarine and the rest of the ingredients except the water in a bowl and mix briskly with a wooden spoon until smooth and fluffy – this will only take a couple of minutes. Gently stir in the water.

3 Tip the mixture on to the syrup and level the surface. Microwave on High (100 per cent power) for 4 minutes until risen and the top is still slightly moist but the sponge is shrinking away from the sides of the dish. Leave to stand for 3 minutes.

4 Tip out on to a plate and serve hot.

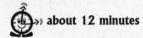 about 12 minutes

BANANAS WITH GOOEY BUTTERSCOTCH SAUCE

You can always store the rest of the sauce in a small container in the fridge and reheat it in the microwave another day.

Serves 2

5 marshmallows
A knob of butter or margarine
1 tbsp golden (light corn) syrup
2 tsp bottled lemon juice
2 bananas

1 Put all the ingredients except the bananas in a bowl. Microwave on High (100 per cent power) for 1 minute. Stir well and leave to stand for 5 minutes.

2 Peel the bananas, split in half lengthways and put on plates. Microwave on High for 30–60 seconds until the bananas are hot but still hold their shape. Spoon the sauce over and serve.

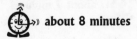 about 8 minutes

---

De-crystallise syrup or honey

Don't throw away the end of a can or jar when the contents have crystallised.

1 Remove the metal lid (if in a jar) or, if in a can, spoon the contents into a bowl or jug. Microwave on Medium (50 per cent power) for 20–30 seconds. Stir well. Add extra 10 second bursts, if necessary, until completely runny.

2 Leave to cool before use. The syrup or honey will thicken again as it cools but the crystals will have gone.

ICE-CREAM WITH HOT CHOCOLATE AND CARAMEL SAUCE

You probably could eat all this sauce in one go, but you might not feel very well afterwards!

Serves 2

1 Mars bar
A knob of butter or margarine
2 tbsp milk
Vanilla ice-cream

1 Break up the Mars bar and put it in a bowl with the butter or margarine and milk. Microwave on Medium (50 per cent power) for about 3 minutes, stirring every minute with a fork or a wire whisk, until smooth and thick. Leave to stand for 2 minutes.

2 Put scoops of ice-cream in two bowls (or one if eating alone) and spoon the hot sauce over.

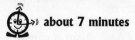 **about 7 minutes**

Chocolate meltdown

Whether you want to melt chocolate to make a dessert, to mix with milk as a hot drink or just to dip pieces of fruit into as a complete luxury, you can do it easily in the microwave.

1 Break up the block into squares and place in a bowl.

2 Microwave on Medium (50 per cent power) for 1–3 minutes, stirring every 30 seconds. Do not overheat or it will burn.

Note: If trying to melt a small quantity (less than ½ a mugful), put a mug with some water in the microwave alongside the bowl to help the chocolate melt without burning.

WARM ALCOHOLIC SNOW

This is really called zabaglione and is very posh to impress
people. Share it with someone special!

Serves 2

1 egg
1 tbsp sugar
1 ½ tbsp whisky, rum, any liqueur or white wine
To serve
Sweet biscuits (cookies)

1 Whisk together the ingredients in a bowl with a wire
whisk.

2 Microwave on Medium (50 per cent power) for
20 seconds, then whisk for a few seconds until the
mixture is beginning to froth. Cook in 10 second blasts
for 1 minute, whisking after each blast until thick and
foamy.

3 Spoon into two glasses and serve with sweet biscuits.
Eat with a spoon.

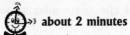 about 2 minutes

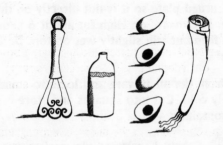

FUDGE BROWNIES

Sticky, moist, chocolatey – great comfort food! Add a handful of chopped walnuts to the mix, if you like.

Makes about 20

½ × 250 g/9 oz block or small tub of butter or margarine
1 × 100 g/4 oz bar of plain (semi-sweet) chocolate, broken into squares
1¼ mugs sugar (preferably soft brown)
4 eggs
1 mug plain (all-purpose) flour
1 tsp vanilla essence (extract)

1 Line the base of a shallow rectangular dish, large enough to hold 3 mugfuls of water, with non-stick baking parchment or greased greaseproof (waxed) paper.

2 Put the butter or margarine, chocolate and sugar in a large bowl and microwave on High (100 per cent power) for 2 minutes, stirring twice, until melted.

3 Beat in the eggs with a wire whisk or a wooden spoon, then stir into the chocolate mixture with the flour and vanilla.

4 Tip the mixture into the prepared dish. Stand the dish on an upturned plate so it is not directly on the turntable. Microwave on High for about 6 minutes or until just firm but still slightly wet on top. Don't overcook!

5 Remove from the microwave and leave to stand until completely cold. Cut into squares and store in an airtight container.

 about 12 minutes, plus cooling time

FRUIT AND NUT MALLOW BARS

These are a simple and delicious variation on the old childhood favourite crispy cakes – they are very moreish!

Makes 12

4 tbsp butter or margarine
1 × 100 g/4 oz bag of marshmallows
2 tbsp clear honey
3 mugs crisped rice cereal
1 × 80 g/3½ oz/small bag of nuts and raisins
Oil for greasing

1 Put the butter or margarine in a bowl and heat on High (100 per cent power) until melted.

2 Snip the marshmallows into small pieces with scissors and add to the bowl. Microwave on High for 1 minute until the marshmallows have melted. Stir briskly until the foamy marshmallow blends with the fat.

3 Stir in the cereal and nuts and raisins.

4 Press into an oiled 18 × 28 cm/7 × 11 in shallow baking tin (or a similar-sized container), pressing down firmly with the back of a wet spoon.

5 Leave until cold and set firm. Cut into bars.

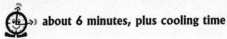 about 6 minutes, plus cooling time

CHOCOLATE CRACKLES

Ring the changes by adding a handful of currants, raisins, chopped nuts or glacé cherries to the mixture.

Makes about 12

¼ × 250 g/9 oz block of butter or hard margarine
3 tbsp golden (light corn) syrup
4 tbsp brown or white sugar
2 tbsp cocoa (unsweetened chocolate) powder
2 mugs cornflakes

1 Put all the ingredients except the cornflakes in a large bowl. Microwave on High (100 per cent power) for 2–3 minutes, stirring every minute, until melted and bubbling.

2 Add the cornflakes and stir until well coated.

3 Either spoon the mixture into paper cake cases (cupcake papers) or spoon in small piles on a lightly oiled plate. Chill until firm. Store in an airtight container.

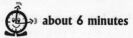 about 6 minutes

---

Refresh stale biscuits

Forgot to put your biscuits (cookies) in a tin? You can crisp them up as follows (but not creams or chocolate-covered ones – they'll melt!):

1 Arrange plain biscuits or crackers side by side in a circle, in a single layer on a sheet of kitchen paper (paper towel) on the turntable or base of the microwave.

2 Microwave on High (100 per cent power) for 40–60 seconds. Leave to stand until cold (they will crisp as they cool). Store in an airtight container.

SHORTBREAD

This is delicious with cups of tea or for dessert with some fresh fruit. Make it as comfort food when you're revising.

Makes 8 wedges

½ × 250 g/9 oz block of butter or hard margarine, plus extra for greasing
¼ mug sugar
1 mug of plain (all-purpose) flour
½ mug cornflour (cornstarch)

1 Put the butter or margarine in a bowl and soften on Low (10 per cent power) for 30 seconds. Work in the remaining ingredients with a wooden spoon or a fork to form a dough, then use your hands to squeeze it together.

2 Lightly smear the centre of a dinner plate with a very little butter or margarine. Press the dough into a round about 18 cm/7 in on the plate. Prick all over with a fork.

3 Microwave on High (100 per cent power) for 4–6 minutes until just firm but still pale. Leave to stand for 5 minutes. Mark into wedges with a knife, then leave to cool completely before cutting.

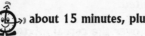 about 15 minutes, plus cooling time

CHOCOLATE CRUNCHY BARS

These are for chocaholics and are great for when you're
studying late.

Makes 12–16

Oil for greasing
¾ × 250 g/9 oz block of butter or hard margarine
4 tbsp sugar (preferably light brown)
3 tbsp cocoa (unsweetened chocolate) powder
2 tbsp golden (light corn) syrup
1 × 500 g/1 lb 2 oz packet of crunchy oat and fruit cereal
1 × 200 g/7 oz bar of plain (semi-sweet) cooking chocolate

1 Oil an 18 cm × 28 cm/7 in × 11 in or similar-sized
shallow rectangular container.

2 Put the butter or margarine, sugar, cocoa and syrup in a
bowl. Microwave on High (100 per cent power) for
1–1½ minutes, stirring once, until melted.

3 Stir in the cereal and press into the container.

4 Break up the chocolate and place in a separate bowl.
Microwave on Medium (50 per cent power) for
3–4 minutes, stirring once or twice and checking every
30 seconds, until melted.

5 Spread the chocolate over the cereal mixture, right to
the corners.

6 Leave until cold, then chill until firm. Cut into fingers
and store in an airtight container.

 about 12 minutes, plus chilling time

PEANUT, FRUIT AND HONEY BITES

Use any cheap brand of biscuits for this recipe – you can even buy broken ones in some stores.

Makes 12

1 × 200 g/7 oz packet of plain biscuits (cookies)
Oil for greasing
3 tbsp butter or margarine
3 tbsp clear honey
3 tbsp peanut butter
A good handful of ready-to-eat dried apricots, chopped, or raisins

1 Put the biscuits in a plastic bag and bash with a rolling pin or bottle until crushed into small pieces.

2 Oil an 18 cm/7 in square or similar-sized shallow container.

3 Put the butter or margarine and honey in a bowl. Microwave on High (100 per cent power) for 1½–2 minutes, stirring twice, until boiling.

4 Stir in the biscuit pieces, peanut butter and chopped apricots or raisins and mix well.

5 Press the mixture into the container, leave until cold, then chill until firm. Cut into squares and store in an airtight container.

 about 8 minutes, plus chilling time

INDEX

INDEX